The Brooklyn Kid II

By

Domenick Scarlato, Ed. D.

The Brooklyn Kid II

© 2019 by Domenick Scarlato, Ed.D.

Cover illustration by Domenick Scarlato, Ed.D.

Dedication

To all who have succeeded in spite of
the obstacles life has presented to them.
God Bless them all and may the future generations
learn from them.

Acknowledgements

I want to thank friends and family who helped

Also, I wish to thank my wife, Laraine, for her support
and valuable assistance.

All my love

Heart and Soul

TABLE of Contents

Introduction

The Brooklyn Kid II is a dramatic story

Of a man who tries desperately to become a success.

After numerous adventures he is forced to decide which

one of two roads he must choose for his future. Does he
make the right choice?

You decide.

ONE
The Decision

It's strange how the clouds shed their tears. They could be on one side of the city or another. In fact, they could be on one side of the street and none on the other side.

So it was with Domenick. He was sitting on his stoop of his apartment while smoking a cigarette. He was contemplating which of the four roads in life to take. The rain came down heavy as a sun-shower with all its drops on the other side of the street. While Domenick sat totally dry, it was strange to see this phenomenon. Domenick asked himself, *"Could this be an omen?"* Could this be help for him to make his decision on which road to choose?

As it was written in the first book, The Brooklyn Kid, a man had to choose one of four roads to happiness.

Four roads. Four roads, but which one? One road is to rejoin the U.S. Navy and have a career as a Chief Petty Officer, or, a second road leading to a singing career for fame and fortune. Could it be the third road to go downtown and join the Navy Street Boys gang and live the fast life with people who believed, "It's a sin to pay for anything"? Or could it be the bliss of marriage, which most of the returning WWII veterans were doing?

Suddenly there was an explosion on the corner of Park Avenue and Classon Avenue, the street on which Domenick lived. It was the paint factory on fire. This explosion shook him back to reality. The flames rose so high in the street they looked like sun. There were screaming fire trucks racing to this horrendous fire. There were at least three fire companies from different neighborhoods. The firemen worked tirelessly for hours to put out this huge fire. Domenick sat mesmerized by this sight, which was only half a block away from where he was sitting.

The rain had stopped, and after many hours the fire department finally put out this horrible fire. Unfortunately there were six people injured and three people killed. This incident brought chills to Domenick's spine and he began to shake. He had reflected to some of his unfortunate experiences he had in the Navy. He quietly regained his composure.

Domenick thought to himself, could this weird rain phenomenon coupled with the fire be an omen for him to wake up and come to a final decision? No, there were no such things as omens, but a decision had to be made now by him and him alone. Love always seems to trump the odds of life. Domenick loved Vickie, his family, and he was brought up in a very traditional manner. He decided to choose marriage, as many WWII veterans were doing. Was this the right decision? This we will see as the future unfolds.

The wedding, as tradition dictated, was that the girl's parents paid for the wedding. Domenick was obligated to furnish the apartment. At the time they announced the wedding, a relative of Vickie's promised them an apartment in a building he owned. This was a time when all the fifteen million veterans coming home were not only seeking jobs but also getting married. Apartments were as scarce as hens' teeth. This promise was a Godsend, but all is not well in Brooklyn. Vickie's brother, Benny, had made his girlfriend pregnant.

She wanted a quick but formal wedding with all the bells and whistles. She even walked down the aisle in a white virgin gown. Vickie's parents paid for Benny's wedding as an appeasement to the pregnant girl. This threw a wrench into Vickie and Domenick's own wedding plans. Now Domenick had not only to pay for the furnishings of an apartment but also the rings, the wedding, the cars, the flowers, reception hall, etc. He had to get the money to pay for the complete wedding plans. Both sides had many relatives — over 400 guests — and all expected to be invited to the wedding. It appeared that this wedding was going to be like a circus. Also to put some gasoline on the fire, it is to be mentioned that a month before the wedding that nice relative who promised Vickie an apartment reneged. He probably got more money in the rent and also "got paid under the table," as a bribe was called in the business world. If Vickie and Domenick were to marry, they would have to move into the "coal water" five room apartment with his parents, brother, and sister. Why move into Domenick's parents' apartment? Well, Benny and his bride moved in with his parents. As it was said, in 1948 apartments were as scarce as hen's teeth, due to the fifteen million veterans coming home. This put a second thought into Domenick's head about getting married. But get married he will! [Figure 1]

Figure 1: Victoria Nigro, 1948

Jobs were scarce as there were millions of veterans looking for work. For Domenick, no one needed his skills in demolition work, nor his skills in machinist work. He was willing to work at any job, whether it be a laborer or whatever.

Rockwood Chocolate Company was a huge processing plant for producing chocolate from the raw beans to a ready processed chocolate. They supplied the bulk chocolate to all the big name companies, such as Fanny farmer, Barracini, etc. These companies would melt the chocolate and pour it into their molds and sell them under their name.

Domenick finally landed a job with the Rockwood Chocolate Factory as a laborer, which was six blocks from his house. As a laborer all you needed was a strong back as you were needed to unload one hundred pound sacks of cocoa beans. There was no "Hi-Lo" to unload the trucks. It was strictly a line of men carrying sacks from the truck to the conveyor belts. At the end of the day you were very tired and you looked like a chocolate man from the powder that came from the sacks. At least Rockwood had showers for the men to take before they went home. Domenick was good worker and ambitious. In one season he moved from the loading dock to the production line where the girls boxed the chocolate products. He made sure the girls never ran out of boxes. By the third season he moved from the production line to becoming a "Temper." A Temper constantly checks the temperature of the cooking chocolate. He also regulates the sizes of the products plus generally inspects the operations of the production line. The job wasn't the best in the world, but it did give Domenick a salary so he could save for his coming marriage.

Would the weekly salary from Rockwood's and some of the savings he had from the Navy pay for the entire wedding? This worried Domenick. With this burden on his mind, he went to seek out his old friends at the Navy Street pool room.

When Domenick arrived at the pool room he went straight to the back room where the "real action" took place. He was greeted with big warm hugs. He then explained his dilemma on the need for money. Mario, who seemed to be the brains of the group, told Domenick there may be a spot for him on a job they were planning. While this discussion took place a man came running into the room. He told the group to put on the radio and listen to the reporting of a hold-up that went bad.

The radio blared out that the police had a fur warehouse surrounded and a shoot-out was in progress. He said it was "Moe-Moe" inside. He said he knew this because he had overheard him and two other men planning the fur heist at this very warehouse. What made this caper go sour was that during the burglary they shot a policeman. As one knows, if you shoot a policeman then you will have the entire twenty-eight thousand police force after you. In those days the cops did not hesitate to shoot to kill. As the radio announcer described the shoot-out bit by bit, it ended up that all three crooks were shot dead. The group was stunned. Each man in the group stared at each other and not a word was spoken. It was completely silent. Domenick got up from his chair and calmly said, "I'll see you guys around." He slowly walked out of the pool room and any thoughts of trying to raise easy money vanished.

Many thoughts had passed through his mind as to what his future should be. Being brought up in a very traditional home with high morals and work ethics, Domenick resigned himself to the fact that hard work was the only way to succeed in life. He vowed to work hard, save his money, get married, and possibly buy a house someday.

Domenick loved his mother and father very much. Consequently he went along with their tradition of having a grand wedding. When he realized that between his mother and Vickie's mother the planning of this wedding will have over four hundred guests, he started to feel that this costly wedding could be a nightmare. The pressure of trying to adjust to civilian life and the planning of this wedding by both mothers was becoming too much for him to handle. Domenick tried to talk to his father for some guidance and help. The only thing he got from his father was that he did not want to get involved, and he told Domenick to let the women handle everything. [Figure 2]

Figure 2: Carmela & Damiano (Tom) Scarlato 1949

The thought of how this wedding would turn out kept Domenick awake at night, but worse was when he did fall asleep were the nightmares he experienced. The shark that brushed along side of him during U.D.T. Frogman training, the articles he found underwater from the dead Soldiers and Sailors at Normandy, and the most traumatizing was being blown out of the water by a nearby exploding mine. Each caused him to be awakened with cold sweats and shaking. It took a number of years for these nightmares to subside. But never entirely.

There were and are many, many veterans who are in worse shape than anyone can imagine. Adjusting to civilian life was a tremendous challenge. For all WWII veterans upon being discharged from the service, the government issued a booklet entitled, "Going Back to Civilian Life." It was the hope that this booklet would help keep veterans out of trouble and adjust to the civilian society. The booklet gave some help, but in reality it had only a small effect.

Domenick's heart has always gone out to his fellow veterans, and he tried whenever he could to help them. He joined the American Legion veterans' organization, which not only provided help to veterans but also provided comradeship. The comradeship helped Domenick cope with civilian life. In years to come he became very active in the Legion program.

Domenick had been a long time member of the Bedford Y.M.C.A., and when he came home from the Navy he rejoined the "Y." He was always physical and wanted to stay in shape. At the YMCA he would "work-out" weight lifting, body building, running the track, punching the big bag, and so on. If there were other members around, he would team-up and play handball or basketball. After a two-hour workout he would always swim in the pool. When he left the "Y" he felt like he could "lick the world."

While attending the YMCA he met two old friends. Angelo "Chisi" Chisano and Harry Diaz were friends when he was only fourteen years old. They used to meet at the YMCA three times a week and not only weight-lifted and body-built together but also socialized.

They loved to talk about when they were teenagers. Chisi, who was tall, handsome, and had long hair with a "D.A." (Duck's Ass), was a little older than Domenick. Harry was short but had a body with such definition that any bodybuilder would want. He was about the same age as Domenick. As they reflected back to 1942 in the warm weather, they would play hooky from school and go to the beach at Coney Island. One day while at Coney Island, Chisi, Harry, and Domenick walked — or for a better word, strutted — along the beach "showing off" their physiques, a hair-raising scream came through the air. A small boy was caught in the surf and was drowning. A mob of people rushed towards the edge of the water, and with that the lifeguard barreled right through the crowd and dove into the surf. The lifeguard was like a shark cutting through water at a rapid but smooth speed. He reached the boy just as he was going down for the third time and he grabbed the boy's hand. The lifeguard finally reached the shore with the unconscious boy. He tried desperately to revive the boy. There were dozens of people in a circle watching the lifeguard trying very hard to save the boy, but unfortunately it was too late. The boy was dead.

Harry, Chisi, and Domenick walked away with dry mouths and some tears in their eyes. Domenick said, "For the Grace of God, there go I." Chisi said, "What did you say?" Domenick answered that this tragedy reminded him of an incident when he was approximately five years old. Chisi asked Domenick what had happened. Domenick started his story by saying when his mother and father took him to Valley Stream Park in Long island, New York, they picnicked on the beach of a large lake. He continued to say that while in the lake he was wading waist deep in the water. He pretended to be a rabbit while hopping on each leg and singing a hippity-hop song. All of a sudden he was engulfed by a large hole at the bottom of the lake. He gasped for air and was swallowing lots of water. He was drowning. Fortunately God was with him. A man came out of nowhere and pulled him out of the water. The man carried him to the shoreline and consoled him. He then left just as he came. Out of nowhere. Domenick ended his story by saying he never knew the man nor his name. "I wish I had." He sometimes wonders if this could have been his guardian Angel. Who knows?

The three eventually drifted apart as Harry got married and moved away. Chisi and Domenick kept their close relationship by double dating. Domenick with Vickie and Chisi with Vickie's best friend, Theresa Scambatti. The relationship between them was like brothers. They were so close that Domenick asked Chisi to be Best Man at his wedding.

Domenick had met an elementary school classmate of his from P.S. 157. His name was Angelo Gargano. Angelo was short but good looking. He loved to talk and talk. He and Domenick, while in the 8th grade, had painted an 8 ft. by 30 ft. mural on the wall of the school's auditorium. The scene depicted mountains, forests, lakes, rivers, sky, and a realistic Indian village. When Domenick had returned home from the Navy he made a visit to P.S. 157. He saw some of his old teachers, who were elated to see him. Mrs. King, the strictest of all his teachers, cried when she hugged Domenick. This brought tears to his eyes.

When he went to the auditorium to see if the mural was still there, he found it still on display and as beautiful as ever.

Angelo and Domenick talked about old times. The good and the bad, but mostly good. During their conversation Angelo told him that he had applied for the Art Scholarship Program that the Pratt Institute, a renowned College of Arts and Architecture, was promoting. They gave a four year scholarship to deserving people who pass their test. Angelo encouraged Domenick to take the test, especially since the Pratt Institute was only four blocks from Domenick's home. Naturally it was on the other side of the tracks, Myrtle Avenue. He had no formal training in the Arts, but Domenick took Angelo's advice and applied for Art Scholarship test. It was a tough test. There were one hundred questions plus one essay question. Also there was an assignment to draw four subjects. One of a landscape with shadowing, etc., an absent-minded professor, a portrait of a person, and the last one, a starving dog. Domenick submitted his final product to the Pratt scholarship committee and waited nervously for their decision.

TWO
Preparation

Domenick saw a need to spruce up his apartment, especially for his upcoming wedding. He first tackled the job of putting a light in the toilet, which was the size of a telephone booth. The toilet never had a light, only a translucent glass as part of the door, which allowed some kitchen light to enter. After he installed the light he replaced the translucent glass on the door with a large mirror. Now when one wants to shave he does not have to look into a small medicine cabinet mirror above the kitchen sink.

He replaced the kitchen's pull-chain light with a fluorescent light with a switch. Domenick painted all the ceilings and woodwork, and then asked his Uncle Nick Misiano to teach him how to wallpaper all five rooms. Last but not least he and his uncle replaced the linoleum on the kitchen floor. The apartment looked spanking new.

The wedding. Oh, the wedding. It could have been

held at the Knights of Columbus hall or the American legion Hall. No, it had to be at the Arion Ballroom. This is what both mothers wanted and this is what they would get.

The Arion Ballroom could hold 480 people, plus it had a stage and balconies. The ballroom was located in Brooklyn on Broadway and Flushing Avenue and it was classy. It was also costly. When Domenick and his parents went to sign the rental contract he was amazed at the size of the hall. It was a sight to behold with its balconies and small stage. Yes, it was a sight to behold and Domenick, being a young novice, accepted it without question.

The next and most important item of the wedding was the rings. Domenick's mother said to him that the best place to buy the wedding and engagement ring is at the Diamond Exchange Center in Manhattan.

The Diamond Exchange center was located in the Bowery section of Manhattan. It was at the foot of the Manhattan Bridge, at canal Street and 2nd Avenue, and it was a series of jewelry stores begging for business. Domenick's mother seemed to favor not the ordinary jewelry store but a store with a number of tables with vendors each hawking their wares. As Domenick and his mother entered this unusual store they were greeted by smiles and waving arms from each vendor. Most vendors were either Jewish or Arab. And some had heavy accents. Domenick felt so embarrassed but he tried to smile back. He felt very awkward because of his ignorance in buying such an expensive item, plus he was troubled by the heavy accents. His mother had no problem as she negotiated the prices from vendor to vendor.

Domenick finally picked out the rings that his mother said were appropriate. She then had them appraised by a vendor who was certified to document both rings' authenticity and as advertised. The vendor who sold Domenick the engagement and marriage rings said that his mother was the toughest of all the customers he ever had. When Domenick figured out the cost of the Ballroom, caterer, the church, limo, etc. he realized that even working overtime on Saturdays he would not have enough money to cover the cost of the wedding. He had to come up with some honest way of getting money.

Domenick thought to himself that the Ridgewood Grove Arena had boxing matches, and they paid good money for fighters. He called Ettore Penn, a former professional heavyweight fighter who had trained him when he was a teenager and boxed in the P.A.L. and C.Y.O amateur matches. Domenick had been a middleweight then and was still a middleweight now.

Incidentally, Ettore Penn fought Tommy Morielle who had in turn knocked down Joe Louis, Boxing Champion of the World, in the first round. Needless to say, Louis knocked out Morielle in the fifth round and retained his title. It is still great to know an individual such as Ettore who was close to being a contender for the World Championship. Unfortunately his fighting career ended as when he talked he kept shrugging his shoulders and moving his head to his right side. In 1944 Ettore had tried to convince Domenick to become a professional fighter but was not successful as Domenick ran off and joined the United States Navy. Now Domenick asked Ettore to help train him and be his Second in his corner at the boxing match. Ettore said he would be in his corner whenever he was needed.

The Ridgewood Grove Arena had six bouts and paid a prize of $50.00 if a fighter lasted the fight. If he lasted the full six rounds he would get $100.00, and if he won the bout he would get $500.00. This was a good incentive for Domenick to fight. His first fight, with Ettore in his corner, lasted six rounds and he got $100. His second fight he won another $100. His third and fourth fights he won, $500 for each. Ettore was elated and said that with more experience Domenick can go to the top. But there was a problem. As one knows, no one can fight six rounds and not get some lumps, as they call them. After each fight, especially the last one, Domenick had some swelling over his left eye and a red face. His mother, and especially Vickie, saw his face and questioned what happened. Domenick tried to avoid the questions, but finally he admitted he was fighting for money. Not only did his mother disapprove of his fighting, but Vickie said she would not marry a professional fighter who will lose his "looks" and become "punch drunk." With this Domenick quit the ring. Ettore Penn was devastated by his decision but understood Domenick's dilemma with his fiancé. He told Domenick that he would always be in his corner anytime he needed him. The prize money he received from the fights helped ease his mind in his coming wedding. By the way, Domenick's father was elated that his son was a boxer and won his fights. But as always, love trumps all.

Domenick finally received the results of the art test

he took for Pratt's scholarship program. Luck was with him as he passed this test with high marks and with remarks that praised his talent and imagination. His luck was short lived. When he went for the interview with a counselor he was questioned about his not having an Academic Regents High School diploma. Domenick stated that he did not have any high school diploma. This fact disqualified him from receiving the four year scholarship. The counselor advised him to possibly go to night school for his diploma. Domenick said he would keep this in mind and left crushed.

There were many disappointments in his life, and this one was devastating. He got drunk that night. But being of strong character, he only drank that one night. Domenick would bounce back to fight more disappointments that life would bring. The night he had gotten drunk brought more trouble for Domenick. He had gone to a bar called the 456 Club, where most of the guys hung out. Domenick was not only disappointed that he did not get the scholarship, he was also very angry. This caused an attitude of hostility which does not serve a man well when he is drinking. There were a number of guys Domenick knew. There were also two men he was not familiar with. The men claimed to be ex-paratroopers from the 101st Screaming Eagles. The men began talking war stories. Somehow, Domenick was asked where he served. He related that he served in the Navy's U.D.T. He explained that U.D.T. stood for Underwater Demolition Team, commonly called "The Frogmen." One of the men was acting quite superior and asked, "What the hell did they do?" Domenick calmly explained the mission of the UDT. The second man said Domenick was full of crap and that there never was a UDT. At this point Domenick was hot as a branding iron, but still trying to compose himself. A few more belittling comments from these ex-paratroopers set him off, and all hell broke loose. When the smoke cleared, so to speak, one man was knocked out and the second man lay moaning with a broken arm. As Domenick knew many of the men in the bar, they covered up for him. They convinced the two men to keep their mouths shut and never to come back. The only trouble was Domenick had to pay the medical bills for the guy's broken arm. This caused Domenick to be short in his savings. No matter, he still had enough money coming in.

The disappointment of not getting the scholarship, because he did not have an Academic H. S. diploma, caused Domenick to think he should go to night school. Even though he only had an elementary school education, which did serve him well, there were times he was held back for lack of a high school diploma. He went to central Evening High School, Girls High School in the daytime, and spoke to a counselor about getting his Academic H. S. diploma. The counselor said to Domenick that he would send for his transcript from Chelsea Vocational High School and would see what could be credited. The next week Domenick saw the counselor who told him that there were no credits which he could use for an Academic diploma, but he could go the General Education Diploma. Domenick said he did not want a G.E.D. He wanted the Academic diploma, which in those days was the top diploma and was needed for college.

The counselor said to Domenick, "You could go four years to night school and then take the State Regents with the kids in the day."

Domenick said he would give it a try. The counselor liked Domenick's determination. He advised him that there is a special program in which he could accelerate the four years into two years. "In other words, you could complete a four year program in only two years. But it takes a lot of time and hard work on your part."

"How can I do this?"

"You must attend four nights a week and take a full year course in one semester. For example, you would take Algebra I and Algebra II in one semester. If you pass the State Regents in that area, you get credit for the whole year. If you fail the Regents, you only get a semester, or half-year credit. So at the end of two years, if you pass all of the required Regents, you get credit for four years and are eligible for an Academic diploma. If you fail the regents, you only get credit for two years. Remember, to make it you must attend four nights per week and study very hard. You think you can do it?"

Domenick replied, the training I had in the Navy qualifies me to do anything. I'll give it a try."

With that Domenick started going to night school while working at Rockwood's. He studied while walking to work, during lunch, in the bathroom, and all his waking hours. He was lucky if he slept four, sometimes five hours a night. Vickie was patient, as he only saw her on weekends for a few hours each day.

THREE
The Wedding

The wedding was scheduled to take place on June 12, 1949, at the St. Lucie Church located on Kent Avenue, Brooklyn. The ceremony was to be held at 5 P.M. sharp. Domenick and Chisi, his best man, were there at 4:45 P. M. Time passed slowly, and at 5 O'clock Domenick asked, "Where is the bride?"

Naturally he did not know that most of the time brides were never on time. Now it was 5:10, and Domenick being a person so regimented to exact time was becoming nervous and agitated. The priest and Chisi tried to calm him and convince him that this was a normal situation. Just as Domenick was about to leave the Alter, Vickie appeared at the entrance of the church. The organist started playing "Ave Maria." The soloist opera singer was William Paulsen, a handsome young blonde tenor and Domenick's 2nd cousin on the Scarlato's side. Domenick was surprised at the music. And Vickie was so beautiful in her wedding gown that he completely forgot about time and his anger. The ceremony went so smoothly and with such emotion that it brought tears to many a person's eyes.

The wedding party left for the photographer's studio and then on to Arion Ballroom for the reception. This ballroom could hold 480 people. At the reception the guard at the door said to Domenick they were already over capacity. How could this be? Well in those days there were no sit down dinners. It was all you could eat sandwiches, all you could drink soda, beer and wine. Cakes, cookies, and other amenities were included. There were families who brought to the wedding not only their immediate family members but also friends and whoever. The ballroom was so packed that they had to open the balcony section to accommodate the people. Everyone had a good time. All you could eat and drink, and the band played great music. The wedding was the talk of the town. To Domenick it was a circus. He could not wait to leave and go on his honeymoon to Lake George, New York.

As fate would have it, the Biology, Mathematics, and History Regents examinations were scheduled to be taken on June 19, 1949. This was right in the middle of Domenick's honeymoon. This was bad enough, but to have all three exams in one day was tough.

When the honeymoon couple took off for Dunham's Bay Lodge in Lake George, Domenick brought along some material to study. At the cabin he said, "The hell with studying." He used his study material to start a fire in the fireplace.

While at the Lodge, Domenick tried not to think about the upcoming Regent exams. He and Vickie tried to enjoy the activities offered at the Lodge—swimming, boating, hiking, archery, and horseback riding. Vickie managed to ride a slow moving horse plus she was real good at and loved archery. [Figure 3]

Figure 3: Victoria Nigro Scarlato 1949

Unfortunately, the sun was not kind to Vickie. She was sunning herself on the dock of the lake, in a bathing suit and without sunscreen protection. Her fair skin was burned red like a lobster. What a thing to happen on a honeymoon. Domenick tried very gently to put on Noxzema cream on her to soothe the burns but with each stroke of his hand she cried.

While Vickie convalesced from her bad sunburn, Domenick took a canoe ride by himself. As he paddled the canoe through the calm waters of the Cove, he thought to himself. *I wonder if I could make it to Diamond Island.* Mr. Dunham had mentioned this island to Domenick in a previous conversation about the lake. He said that on this small island is a large monument commemorating the Revolutionary War. Diamond Island was about three-quarters of a mile from the cove and out into the main part of the lake. It is to be noted that Lake George was about thirty miles long and ten miles wide. It was like an ocean.

Domenick was getting bored with paddling the canoe in the very calm cove, so he said to himself that he would try to get to the island. He always looked for challenges and a challenge he will find. When paddling the canoe beyond the cove he found the waters in the main part of the lake quite rough, but he pushed onward. After some effort he made it to Diamond Island.

He beached the canoe and searched the island for the monument. When he found it he was very impressed. It was a large column of stone, 20-feet high and 2-feet wide. The inscription described and gave dates of the French and Indian War and the Revolutionary War. Yes it was impressive, especially on such a small island.

When Domenick tried to return to Dunham Bay Lodge he found the waters of the lake were getting even rougher. The canoe needed paddling with more effort. He finally reached the cove but currents and wind prevented him from entering. No matter how hard he paddled he could not make any progress. He removed his shirt to cool off and collected his thoughts. *Could this be the end?* The canoe did take on water and he was getting fatigued from the long hard paddling.

Finally Domenick wised up. *You can't beat Mother Nature, but you can use her.* He figured if he allowed the canoe to drift with the current and he steered with the paddle, he would eventually go diagonally towards the shore opposite the cove. He would land one half, or, a full mile away from the cove. *So be it.* That is what he did. By following the current he eventually landed three-quarters of a mile away. Domenick docked the canoe and washed his face and hands. He threw his shirt over his shoulder and held it with one finger as he walked on the road back to Dunham's Bay Lodge.

While walking on the road he began to sing a song called "Marching Along." A pickup truck pulled up alongside of him. The occupants of the truck were two pretty girls.

One of the girls asked, "What is a handsome guy doing walking around naked?"

"I'm not naked, just hot."

The girls further questioned him as to where he was going. He told them he was headed to Dunham's bay

Lodge where he was staying. The girl driving the truck asked if he wanted a lift. Domenick gladly took the offer as he was very tired from his canoe trip. While in the pickup truck, the girl next to him asked how he came to be on the road. Domenick told them the whole story of his adventurous trip. Both girls laughed and said he was crazy to try such a stunt, but they admired him for surviving.

While Domenick was gone from the lodge everyone was concerned that he did not return. Mr. Dunham and another man took a speed boat and went searching for him. Vickie stood on the dock worried and waiting nervously for some news.

After what seemed like an eternity, Domenick appeared at the Lodge in a pickup truck with two beautiful girls. Vickie's worries were over, but she was burning with rage as she saw the sight of what appeared to be a good time.

It took a while for Domenick to explain what happened. After she heard this story she calmed down and forgave him. However, she said, "Even though you still have three months to be twenty-one, you are now a married man! A married man with the responsibility to take care of both of us!"

She made him promise not to do any more crazy stunts. This was a difficult task, but Domenick kept his promise.

The time came for Vickie and Domenick to

reluctantly leave Lake George. He had to go back to the City to take the rigidly scheduled three Regents tests. Domenick could not miss nor fail taking these tests. He had worked too hard all year attending evening classes. He was scheduled to take the Biology, Mathematics, and History Regents tests at Erasmus High School in Flatbush, Brooklyn, with the kids from the daytime school. Each test was two hours long.

After a beautiful weekend at Lake George, Vickie and Domenick took a Greyhound Bus to New York City and registered in a Sheraton Hotel. Early the next morning Domenick went by subway and then a bus to Erasmus High School. He was very nervous and felt awkward sitting among all those kids. Some of them looked at him like he did not belong. No matter, he took his tests and passed with flying colors. In fact, the evening math teacher, Mr. Kaplan, told Domenick he did not think he could pass the math Regents. Even though Domenick was good in Geometry and Algebra, Mr. Kaplan felt he was weak in Intermediate Algebra. This may seem strange, but Mr. Kaplan made a special visit to Domenick's home to tell him he had passed the regents. Domenick was not home but his father was. Domenick's father was in seventh heaven every time he told the story how the math teacher came to the house. After Domenick took the tests he met Vickie, who had done some shopping on Fifth Avenue.

Domenick had tried his best to go back to Lake George, but Vickie said she always wanted to visit Washington, D.C. She was so insistent that Domenick finally agreed. He said he would be her tour guide. He knew his way around Washington as he was stationed there in 1946 while in the Navy.

They stood at the famous Commodore Hotel

where some of the Congressmen stayed. It is too bad that they did not meet any of their congressmen, but they did visit all the historical sights Washington had to offer. [Figure 4]

Figure 4: Vickie & Dom 1949

The week melted away fast as they enjoyed the sights. Naturally Domenick avoided his old haunts. There was one sight which caused Domenick to pause and reflect. A little colored boy was selling peaches on Constitution Avenue. Domenick's mind went back to when he was eleven years old and sold shopping bags in downtown Brooklyn during Christmas week. The DeLeo brothers, Nicky, Frankie, and Rico, were older than Domenick. They told him where to get shopping bags and how to sell them. Domenick needed money to buy his mom, his dad, brother, and baby sister a present. So there he was in the snow on Fulton Street outside of May's Department Store selling his bags. He remembers well how the cops would take your bags, take your money, and chase you away. When you saw a cop you ran like the wind or hid if you can.

After a few very cold evenings of selling, Domenick got a bright idea. Instead of standing with all your shopping bags, have only one in your hand. Then you would say to a passing shopper, "This is my last shopping bag, and it's only five cents." This gimmick worked. He sold all of his bags in no time. The Deleo brothers could never figure out how he sold all his bags so fast. Domenick was able to buy each member of his family a small present. Too bad his father kept strongly questioning him as to where did he get the money for the presents. When he finally told his father how he got the money, he was scolded for going a mile from the house in the snow to sell shopping bags. Domenick never sold anything on the streets again. A horn blew from a passing car, bringing Domenick back to reality. He purchased a bag of peaches from the little boy, plus gave him a tip.

Domenick had told Vickie how shocked he was when he was in the Navy that Washington, D.C. was segregated. That was in 1946. Now in 1949 there was no segregation.

Vickie said to Domenick, "I thought you said there was segregation. I see colored people walking everywhere and in stores. Were you kidding me?"

"I wasn't kidding," he replied. "But something happened to make the Capital what it should be. It should be an example of equality and freedom throughout our land. I'm glad it changed."

FOUR
Naval Air Corps

The honeymoon couple finally arrived back in Brooklyn. They had to move into Domenick's parent's apartment. A five room apartment with five people is not the best way for newlyweds. It was awkward. Adjustments had to be made. Domenick could adapt to this situation. He would be working during the day and attend school in the evening. For Vickie it was awkward. When she finished work she would go to her parents' house and then later in the evening go to be with Domenick. To help relieve the crowded apartment, Christina, Domenick's 10 year old sister, went and stayed around the corner with her grandparents. [Figure 5]

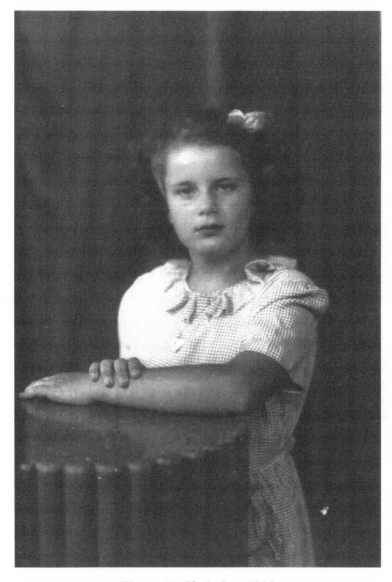

Figure 5: Christina 1950

After about six months, Domenick's parents realized this was not a good situation and began to look for a house. After much effort they purchased a beautiful nine room house in Hollis, Queens. When they moved out Domenick kept the apartment. Even though it was a coal-water flat with a converted kerosene oil heating stove, which heated the five rooms in the winter, it was theirs to do as they chose. It was fun to slowly furnish the apartment, plus it was close to Central Evening High School and their jobs.

Domenick finally graduated from Central H. S. in June 1950. He did get his Academic Regents High School Diploma in two years. At the evening graduation ceremony only Vickie was in attendance. Not one of the parents could make it. Vickie's parents were living in Bellrose, Domenick's parents in Hollis. Domenick did not really care as long as Vickie was there and he got his diploma. To show that he was still naïve about some things, when he went up on stage to receive his diploma, he opened it and it was blank. He was getting upset that he did not get his diploma. Vickie explained to have the real diplomas on the stage may get the names mixed up and some people get someone else' diploma. To solve this they give out blanks and the real diplomas come in the mail. Domenick understood the reasoning but he was still disappointed. He had worked very hard for this moment and was anxious to see what an Academic High School diploma really looked like.

The counselor who had originally directed Domenick into the two-year program was present at the graduation ceremony. He congratulated him for his accomplishment and advised him to go on to college. He knew Domenick had served in the Navy and was entitled to three years of education under the "G.I. Bill." He told Domenick to stop in and see him some night and they could talk about him attending New York University. He said, "With your ability and determination, you should go on to higher education. Don't waste your talents."

Domenick went to see the evening school counselor for advice on which college to attend and also what could be his major. The counselor suggested that he enroll at New York University because of a number of reasons. Domenick loved the outdoors, the mountains, the ocean, and nature as a whole. The counselor suggested he major in Geology.

"You'll work outdoors, travel, and could even minor in oceanography." He knew Domenick was fascinated with underwater terrains and marine life.

Another reason was that N.Y.U. was a top rated university, and it was close to home. The University was right over the Manhattan Bridge, in Greenwich Village. The counselor suggested that he attend classes in the day time and save part of his allowance to complete the four year course. Domenick only had three years under the G.I. Bill. He had thought about majoring in Art, but he remembered being told that fine artists starve and commercial art is like a closed profession. He took the counselor's advice and will major in Geology,

Unfortunately Vickie was "laid off" from her job. For Domenick to attend daytime at N. Y. U. was impossible with the small allowance the government would provide. Vickie, for whatever reason, decided not to look for another job. She said it was a woman's prerogative that when she is married she didn't have to work. Although this upset Domenick, being a traditional person he accepted this situation. He decided he would work in the day and attend evening classes. It would take longer, but he was used to going to night school. He did it for two years at Central Evening. H. S.

During the early spring of 1950, the world was in such turmoil that Domenick decided to join the Navy Air Corps Reserve. He told Vickie that if another World War broke out. He and many veterans would be called back into the Service. He said he had served in the Navy Underwater with the U.D.T. and on top of the water on a destroyer. Now he wanted to serve in the air. Domenick had always loved aviation. As a boy he drew pictures of planes, made model airplanes, and originally tried to study aviation but went to the wrong school for that program. He told Vickie the reserves meet one weekend each month but are home every night. Also, they train for two weeks in the summer. All of his training would be done at Floyd Bennet Field in Brooklyn, close to home. The extra money for drill meetings would come in handy. Domenick also had convinced Salvatore, his seventeen year old brother, a good looking boy, to join the reserves with him. [Figure 6]

Domenick Scarlato, Ed.D

Figure 6: Salvatore 1950

Domenick was assigned to the Grumman "Avenger" TBF bomber squadron. The weekend training sessions were indeed held at Floyd Bennet Field, and the summer maneuvers were conducted aboard CVA 41 carrier, the Midway. It is a coincidence that Domenick when serving aboard the destroyer Larson DD830 five years earlier had escorted the Midway. Now he is serving and flying off this same carrier. Domenick served as a rear Machine Gunner. When not flying he worked as an Aviation Mechanic A1/C. His brother, Salvatore, went through boot camp and was assigned to the same squadron as Domenick. It is believed that Sal did not like flying, because his first flight was scary. He was scheduled to be in the same plane as Domenick but something "screwed up." Explicitly, when Sal and Domenick were issued their parachutes, Sal did not know how to strap it on. The planes in the squadron were already warming up on the tarmac. Domenick worked frantically to correctly put the parachute on Sal and give him instructions on its use. The planes were not taking off and the plane that Domenick and Sal were assigned to was the flight Commander's plane. Traditionally the first plane to take off would be the flight Commander. But the flight Commander's plane was still on the ground. All the planes could not wait because they were using up fuel. Consequently, all were taking off before the Commander. Sal and Domenick raced towards the Commander's plane. Domenick was still trying to put on his chute on the run. In doing so he grabbed the wrong ring and the chute opened. It billowed open from the force of the wind from the airplanes' propellers. It was a very comical sight, Domenick running while deflating the chute. He managed to get it deflated and bundled up.

He ran to the parachute shack and asked for another chute. All of the men from other squadrons really ribbed Domenick with all kinds of cute names. Meanwhile, the parachute rigger told Domenick, "Sorry, only one chute to a customer."

This meant that he could not go on this flight. Without a chute you cannot take a "hop." Domenick was so embarrassed he could have killed himself. When he looked at the field he saw all of the planes circling, waiting for the flight Commander, whose plane was still on the ground. He ran like a race horse. Sal was sitting in the rear radioman's seat. The plane could not takeoff unless the pilot could communicate with the crew and Sal did not know how to operate the intercom system.

Domenick gave him a crash course. When Domenick made contact with the Commander/pilot there are no words that can be repeated as to what the Commander said to him. The plane took off. The squadron was gone for about five hours. They went on a bombing run at Cherry Point.

Domenick had cold sweats for two reasons. One on how his brother made out. Two, he knew he was going before the Commander and be chewed out from head to toe. The squadron returned in good order. Salvatore got out of the plane and looked like a ghost. He said the ride was violent with twists and turns and dives. He didn't know what was going on and he got sick. "I'm going to apply for ground crew. These pilots are crazy." It is to be noted that later that year Salvatore got a release from the Navy so he could join the Marines with his friends from the neighborhood. This was a move which he later regretted. The Korean War broke out and he was shipped to Korea.

He sent letters to Domenick asking, "How can I get out of this 'chicken-shit outfit'?" Domenick was helpless but tried to encourage Sal to make the best of it and listen to the "old timers." Many night Domenick cried for his brother and prayed for him to be all right.

The "snafu" that happened with the parachute caused Domenick plenty of grief. Not only did the flight Commander chew him out like a dog on a bone, but he gave him twenty hours of extra duty to clean out all the airfield's grease pits. Domenick was reassigned to another plane.

A problem arose when he had to enroll at N.Y.U. Domenick was scheduled to have surgery on his right foot at the Veterans Administration Hospital in Brooklyn on August 20, 1950. The deadline for enrollment at N.Y.U. was August 30. He could not cancel the surgery as it had taken over three years to have the government correct a wrong done to him in 1947.

When Domenick was stationed in Washington, D. C. he served in the Navy's Seamen Honor Guard. The Seamen Honor Guard was a highly respected outfit because they stand a two-hour watch at the Tomb of the Unknown Soldier. They attend ceremonies for dignitaries and act as a burial detail at Arlington Cemetery. Their hours were only Nine to Five and they got weekends off. This sounded very good to Domenick as he accepted the assignment. To stand his watch at the Tomb of the Unknown Soldier was a great honor. At that time the service used a Soldier, a Sailor, and a Marine to guard the Tomb, but it changed through the years. Only the Army stands watch now. To perform his duties at the Tomb and at Arlington Cemetery, Domenick had to practice with his fellow Guardsmen on a daily basis. They had to be the sharpest looking men in the service, and Domenick loved it.

One day while standing in formation, a deuce-and-a-half truck backed up and hit Domenick with its rear wheel, knocking him to the ground. In the process the rear wheel went over his right foot. Everyone in the squad yelled and the truck stopped. Good thing the truck stopped as it could have crushed Domenick. He was taken to Bethesda Naval Hospital in Maryland to be treated. They x-rayed his ankle and diagnosed that he had bad contusions and lacerations. He was lucky the ground had been dirt and not concrete as he would have no foot. Domenick's wounds were bandaged and he was sent back to the Receiving Station on crutches. After about three weeks on crutches he went to the sick bay and complained that when he walked he felt something protruding under his right foot. The corpsman said he was developing a callous. After a few visits for the same condition, the corpsman asked a doctor to examine Domenick's foot. The doctor, who was an Ensign, looked at his foot from about two feet away and said it was a Plantar Wart and to cut it off. The corpsman cut away the callous. Even though Domenick continued to complain that there was something protruding from his foot, the diagnosis of an Ensign-doctor was etched in stone. This would plague Domenick for years to come.

What was not known is that at Bethesda Naval Hospital they did not x-ray his whole foot but just his ankle. If they had x-rayed the whole foot they would have found that there were dislocated and crushed metatarsal head and falange, and that there was a bone or bones protruding from under his right foot. They had performed an incomplete diagnosis of his condition and the doctor completely misdiagnosed his condition as being a Plantar Wart. Domenick was not a wimp who would complain. He learned to live with the condition and the constant pain. As we well know in the service, if you go to sick bay too much you are a malingerer, and if you complain you are a wimp. Consequently, you try to overcome and go on as best you can.

Upon being discharged from the U.S. Navy Domenick was entitled to "G.I. Veterans benefits." How did he know about the veterans Administration and benefits? It was from the Pvt. John Spatafore Post of the American legion where he was a charter member. John Spatafore, a handsome husky man, was his first cousin who had enlisted in the U. S. Army at the age of eighteen. He served with the Combat Engineers of the Yankee Division in the initial invasion of Normandy on June 6, 1944. Johnny was killed in action on June 25. Johnny had been raised with Domenick and was like a big brother to him. They went to movies, played together, and shared secrets as close brothers do. Domenick took Johnny's death very hard. He has Johnny's 8"x10" framed picture on his wall. He had Johnny's name and his own name on the Normandy Wall in France, and had both names registered with the WWII Memorial in Washington, D.C. Domenick is an original charter member of the WWII Memorial.

As was previously mentioned, when Domenick was in the Navy he had his right foot injured while serving with the Honor Guard in Washington, D. C. The crushed right foot, misdiagnosed by an Ensign Doctor, plagued him with constant pain. The metatarsal bone that was protruding beneath his foot caused a callous which became more unbearable. He went to the VA to be examined and put in a claim for his injury. Since there were thousands upon thousands of veterans seeking benefits, the lines and waiting periods were enormous. Domenick was finally examined by a high ranking doctor in 1948. The doctor concluded that he needed surgery to correct the protruding bone and other crushed bones in his right foot. He was put on a waiting list to be admitted to the V. A. Hospital. It took two years to be admitted.

Domenick entered the hospital on August 20, 1950 for surgery. He was very concerned that he would not be able to enroll at New York University in time for the fall semester. Time to him was very important. He was on a roll from just graduating Central Evening H. S. and did not want to lose his motivation for school. He had to be at NYU to enroll by August 30. His anxiety about the surgery grew as he stood around waiting for his turn to go to the operating room. At that time the only way to enroll at NYU was in person and after seeing a counselor. You could not enroll by mail. In one day you had to see a counselor, choose your subjects, enroll, and pay the Bursar. This takes time and the lines are long. Domenick was operated on August 25. He had to convince the doctor that he must be released from the hospital before August 30. Dr. Foreman, who had performed the surgery, was reluctant but did sign a release for Domenick.

He left the hospital on crutches, his foot swollen and in terrific pain. His father-in-law, Frank Nigro, drove Domenick and Vickie to NYU in Manhattan. Where he began the process of enrollment in the School of Arts and Sciences. It was an extremely painful day. He stood in line on his own accord while barely negotiating the crutches. Classes started the following week and he attended them while still on crutches. He had to walk three blocks to the subway, change trains, and walk two long blocks to NYU for his classes. All on crutches.

Even though the surgery was supposed to correct the problem with his right foot, Domenick had to wear an orthopedic support for the rest of his life. A callous still formed on the bottom of his foot and had to be periodically removed.

Could the operation on Domenick's foot be a curse or a godsend? After he enrolled at NYU and still on crutches, Chisi drove him to the Naval Air Station at Floyd Bennett Field in Brooklyn. When they arrived Domenick reported that he had to be excused from drills because of his recent surgery. He was shocked that his entire squadron was activated to Korea. The squadron was sent to Korea aboard the U.S.S. Midway.

He later found out that the Avengers had the highest rate of casualties as any other aircraft. While on bombing missions the Avengers were attacked by MIG jet fighters. It need not be said but a propeller-driven plane is no match for a jet fighter; consequently, they were shot down easily. Yes, Domenick thought to himself that the surgery may have been a godsend. He survived a second time in a war.

FIVE
New York University

To reflect back when Domenick went to enroll at NYU, he had to see a counselor who would explain the program and schedule his classes. The Counselor, Professor Baron, told Domenick that to obtain a Bachelor's degree he must follow the required courses for the first two years. The last two years he would pursue his major and minor. The professor scheduled his two three-credit classes, which meet one hour each, two nights per week.

Domenick asked, "Why can't I take two classes each night?" This would give him twelve credits for the semester.

"Such a schedule would be almost like being a full time student. It would be too much for you to handle."

Domenick explained that he had just completed a four year academic high school Regent' program within two years, attending classes four nights per week for two years. He felt confident that if he could do it, he would be able to handle twelve credits. After much discussion the counselor/professor compromised and approved three classes, which were nine credits. Those classes were English, mathematics, and Ancient History. By coincidence, his mathematics teacher would be Professor Baron.

When Domenick started to attend classes he found that he may have bitten off more than he could chew. He did very well with the History class, and in Math he bumped along, the English class was horrible. Plus, in his first week of the English class he was shocked. The teacher, Mrs. Warnke, was a young beautiful woman, with shiny black hair, blue eyes, and a model's figure. She stood at the blackboard on a raised platform, which looked like a stage. As she lectured she never stood still. She moved back and forth as if she were performing on a stage.

At the first class session Mrs. Warnke handed out test sheets, consisting of ten questions on grammar and one which required writing a short essay on a recently read book. When Domenick handed in the test sheet he was shaking. He will not know the results until the next week.

Domenick finally received his English test results from his first class. It was bad. Very bad. This grade was an "F" and the remark on the paper was "very bad grammar." This should not have surprised him as he did not even remember what a noun was. But he still felt depressed. He told himself that he was destined to fail this course. He should drop out of the class. At NYU the policy was that if you already attended one class then you must get permission from the teacher to drop out. If you don't get permission then you will be charged for the course. If you do get permission then you will be reimbursed. This policy for getting the refund forced Domenick to see Mrs. Warnke with the hope of getting her permission. To approach Mrs. Warnke and ask her consent to drop the class was a nerve wracking proposition for him. But this he had to do.

Speaking with her, she asked how did he ever get into NYU. Domenick explained the whole story as to how he had obtained an Academic Regents High School diploma. Mrs. Warnke was very impressed and said to him not to drop out of her class. She said that although his grammar was bad, his writing of the composition had a flare which she liked. She said he had potential. She suggested to improve his grammar he could enroll in a non-credit English remedial course which is given on Saturday mornings. The professor who teaches this course, she said, was professor Sipriano — "…and believe it or not she teaches the course 'Pro Bono. Domenick, with your determination, your experience, and writing potential, you can pass my class."

Domenick took her advice and did not drop her class. He enrolled in the remedial English class.

When he met professor Sipriano, she was already impressed with him. Mrs. Warnke had talked to her about Domenick. Professor Sipriano was a kind middle aged woman who was devoted to helping students in need. His relationship with her was very good. Her class was hard, with the work books and all, but it did help Domenick a great deal. He would remain eternally grateful.

In Mrs. Warnke's class he slowly moved up in grade each week. To Domenick a "C" grade was like an "A". Mrs. Warnke agreed. He went from a "D" to a "D+"

to a "C", and to a "B". His final grade was a "C". He felt like he had gotten an "A". Mrs. Warnke agreed. In his other courses he did very good. In Mathematics he got a "C" and in Ancient History he made "B+"

It was a tough semester but it did boost Domenick's morale to try harder. Try harder he did.

The next semester he was fortunate again to get Mrs. Warnke as his teacher. She was not partial. She was fair. He respected that trait. He admired Mrs. Warnke. Her looks, mannerisms, and intellect fascinated him. It would appear that he had a crush on her. But both of them were married. If they had both been single — who knows?

This second class was English Literature. It required a lot of reading books such as *Dante's Inferno, Paradise Lost, Brave New World,* etc. Critiques of these types of books, and compositions, were detailed and lengthy. It was a tough subject, but Domenick prevailed and completed the course with a "C+". His two other classes were Psychology ("C") and American History (an "A"!).

While attending classes in his second year at NYU, a very tragic incident occurred at the West 4th Street Subway Station in Manhattan. Domenick saw a man fall off the opposite side of the platforms and onto the tracks. A train could be heard coming fast along the same tracks. The poor soul frantically tried to climb back onto the platform when the train came roaring into the station. The man was caught between the side of the train and the platform. The clearance between train and platform was about four inches. The man spun around and around like a rag doll being flung into the air. His arms swirled like blades of a fan and his red blood spattered on the train were like spots on a leopard. Domenick was stunned and paralyzed. He stared at the twisted body for what seemed like an eternity. Finally he shook his head, blinked, and walked away. There was nothing he could do.

As a diversion from critiquing a book, Mrs. Warnke allowed her students to write a story about an exciting incident which they had experienced. Domenick wrote about "The Man on the Subway." Mrs. Warnke was impressed at the surrealistic way Domenick described the incident. She said it reminded her of Jack London's style of writing. She gave him a C+.

Mrs. Warnke's husband was a professor at Columbia University. She said to Domenick that her husband had been following "your career," as he put it, for the past year. "He would very much like to meet with you someday."

Domenick nervously replied, "It would be a pleasure."

At the end of the semester Mrs. Warnke invited Domenick and his wife to her "Bon Voyage party." She and her husband were going to Italy for the summer. Domenick was elated to receive such an invitation. The party was held at 222 Park Avenue, Manhattan. The building had a Doorman and an Elevator Operator. This was real class. Domenick and Vickie were not used to this environment. The nervous couple met with Mrs. Warnke, the professor, and other intellectual people. They slowly fitted in and did earn favorable impressions. Near the end of the night. The professor, Mrs. Warnke's husband, said to Domenick, "Since you have a flare for writing, why not pursue creative writing courses?"

Domenick thanked him for his advice, and explained that his goal was to become a geologist.

At the end of the evening, Mrs. Warnke and the

professor thanked the departing couple for their visit, and said they were always welcome in their home. At that time this was the best compliment that Vickie and Domenick ever received.

Vickie always wanted a baby. She constantly reminded Domenick she would like to have a baby to keep her company when he was at school. He always asked her to please be patient and wait until he finished school. The most important thing for him was to finish school and become a geologist. Everything else was secondary. Time was important, as he not only worked fulltime but carried a heavy load of credits each semester. His home was close to NYU and he looked for work close to home.

His father, Damiano Scarlato, constantly hounded Domenick to take Civil Service exams so as to have a steady and secure job. To appease his father, he took the Department of Sanitation's competitive examination. The written part wasn't too difficult but they made the physical performance part tough. Domenick always kept himself in tip-top shape so this exam was easy for him. Over fifteen thousand took the exams. Domenick came out number 580 on the list. His father was so elated that he told all of his friends. He said, "My son could be Borough Superintendent in no time."

Each time he was called for a position as Sanitation Man, Domenick declined. His father was furious. But Domenick's goal was to finish at NYU. If he didn't finish he could always take the department exam again. Deep down, he didn't want to be a Sanitation man—a garbage man—like his father. He respected his father but he always remembered something his grandfather told him. Each generation must do better than the last generation. Domenick determined to follow that advice.

On July 4, 1953, a healthy blonde 9lb. 8oz. beautiful baby girl, named Toni Carmela Scarlato was born. She was born at 4 O'clock in the afternoon, had four letters in her first name, and represented the 4th generation. Put these facts together and they add up to the number "4." It is obvious that Toni's lucky number should be 4. Toni brought much joy to the Scarlato home, yet in the real world it was an awakening for Domenick. The birth was costly. In those days there were no health care/hospitalization plans. The cost of the birth took all the money they had saved for NYU tuition.

Domenick worked as an Engineering Clerk at Self-Winding Clock Company. The pay wasn't so good but the job was close to home. A woman engineer, named Virginia Bianco, befriended Domenick and always gave him good advice. He admired her so much as she was a woman engineer of Italian descent. When Toni was born, Virginia made a bundle of pink ribbons with many little baby dolls hanging from them. It was a gift to be placed on the baby carriage. This was a fine gesture which made Vickie and Domenick very happy.

After Toni was born, Domenick was forced to stop classes at NYU. He had attended evening classes, winters and summers, for three years while working full time. He had carried anywhere from nine to twelve credits per semester. This was a heavy load and he spent all of his waking hours studying. He had accrued seventy credits before he had to stop. His "G.I. educational benefit" ran out. Plus the expense of his new born baby took all of his savings.

Domenick saw an advertisement in the newspaper that the Department of Defense was having a nationwide federal competitive exam for apprentices to be employed at the New York Naval Shipyard. He tried to reason things out logically. He knew there were opportunities to become an apprentice if he could pass the announced Civil Service examination. Since he was a boy Domenick worked at many jobs. He knew the empty feeling one experiences when one is "laid off" with a real depressed feeling of being unemployed. The responsibility of having a wife and a child was a rude awakening for him. Domenick realized he needed a steady job. The Navy Yard could provide some job security, steady income, a good "Trade," and the Yard was close to home. Also, if he saved enough money maybe, just maybe, he may go back to NYU. He decided to take the Apprentice examination and possibly build a career for himself and his family.

Domenick applied and was scheduled to take the Apprentice test a month later. The test was to be an eight hour exam taken in two sessions, the first in the morning, and the second in the afternoon. It was a multiple choice test with two essays at the end. The test covered every subject imaginable, such as science, mathematics, humanities, logic, government, aptitude, etc. When Domenick entered the classroom where the test was to be taken he saw a room packed with candidates. Two Proctors were there to administer the test. One Proctor gave the instructions on the rules. The other Proctor walked up and down the aisles to monitor and see that no one cheated. It was a nerve-wracking situation. Domenick's hands were sweating and he occasionally had to take a deep breath. He answered every question and finished the test on time. At the end, he was confident that he had passed. He said to himself if it wasn't for NYU he would never have completed the test. Now he had to wait for the results.

One month after Toni was born Domenick's brother, Salvatore, came home from the Marines after serving in Korea during the War. Everyone was joyous and happy that he came home safe and sound. Sal and Vickie's sister Theresa, christened Toni at the St. Lucy Church on Kent Avenue, Brooklyn. Both Sal and Theresa were very happy to be chosen Godfather and Godmother for Toni. The celebration after the christening was held at 177 Classon Avenue. Everyone in the family came to the party. There were over thirty people, and though crowded everyone had a good time.

Baby Toni brought much joy to the Scarlato home. Her first birthday was a real celebration on the 4th of July, with fireworks and all the gala of the holiday. It was a special for two reasons. Toni was their first baby born and it was the 4th of July. Vickie and Domenick decorated the apartment with flags and streamers. Red, white, and blue was everywhere. It was a very patriotic birthday. Domenick had managed to save enough money to buy a Keystone 8mm movie camera and he took many pictures at the party. The apartment was crowded but he got everyone in the movie film. It was a memorable occasion.

Every year afterwards, Toni's father and mother made sure her birthday was celebrated with patriotic paraphernalia and the entire family.

Salvatore was discharged from the United States Marine Corps and his adjustment to civilian life again was as difficult as any veteran encountered. Even though he had a girlfriend, named Theresa, he could not or would not face the future. He would not talk about looking for a job, possibly going to school, or even marriage. His attitude was "The hell with it." Domenick understood Sal's problems and he patiently had numerous brotherly talks with him. Sal confided in his brother. Domenick was becoming Sal's counselor. He didn't want Sal to make the same mistakes he had made and end up "short changing" himself. He took a day off from work and took Sal to the Veterans Administration to put in a claim for battle fatigue (nervousness). He told Sal no matter what the V.A. says you must be consistent in your actions and persistent for your claim. "Do not give up." Domenick also took a day off to go with Sal to the Employment Office so Sal could file for the "52/20" for unemployed veterans. The 52/20 was a G.I. benefit in which a veteran could get $20.00 each week for up to 52 weeks.

During this period of time Sal was living in Hollis with his parents, but all of his friends were in Brooklyn in the old neighborhood. When Sal went out he stayed out until the wee hours of the morning and it would be too late and too long of ride to go home to Hollis. So he would sleep on the couch at Domenick's home. These activities of Sal were very disturbing to his mother and father. Sal's father made a deal with him to buy a good used car so he could come home each night. Sal's mother would be happy. Sal asked Domenick to help him find a good used car. At this time Domenick had a 1951 Chevrolet Hard

Top and he took Sal out each night for three weeks to find a car. They would travel along Hillside Avenue and along Queens Blvd. In those days there were numerous car dealers on these main streets of Queens. At the end of three weeks they finally found a used car which was in great shape, and the price was right. It was a 1948 Chevrolet convertible and it was a beauty. Black with white wall tires, the convertible top was white. The car was almost like new and it checked out perfectly. Sal was very happy and couldn't thank Domenick enough for his help and patience.

Domenick knew Sal was serious with Theresa and wanted to marry her, so he spoke to his brother about going to school full time during the day. Domenick knew from his own experience how tough it was to be married and go to school at night. He knew Sal would never do this. After Domenick did some serious research on occupations and schools, he concluded that since Sal did not have a high school diploma, it would be wise for him to go to a school which gives individual instructions. This school was called Delahanty's. The school prepared individuals to pass civil service tests, and it also taught the occupation of drafting. Its 2,000 hour course, one year full time, prepared a student to be a draftsman. Domenick advised Sal to enroll in this school under the G.I. Bill, which would pay for the entire tuition plus give him a monthly allowance. Sal's father encouraged him to attend. "I have heard of this school and it is good."

Domenick went with his younger brother to the school. Sal enrolled in the Drafting program. This was a move which Sal never regretted as he made drafting his career. After he graduated from Delahanty's Sal obtained a Junior Draftsman's position with the help of a boy friend of his sister Christina. This friend was a red head named John Hegdal. Sal had now settled down and was ready to get married. He and Theresa Cochignano were married in style, and Domenick was his best man.

SIX
New York Naval Shipyard

When Domenick finally received the notice that he passed the Apprentice exam, he was surprised and happy at the results. Over 3,500 applicants nationwide had applied and taken the test. Only 1,800 passed this very difficult and tedious test. Eight hours long with batteries of questions. If an applicant had less than a 95% grade he was not considered for the position. Domenick's education from Central Evening High School plus his successful courses at New York University enabled him to attain a grade of 98.8%. There were only 250 candidates appointed and Domenick was one of them. He was assigned to the Welding Department as an Apprentice Welder-Combination Mechanic, with a starting salary of $60.00 per week. He was to work in the Brooklyn Navy Yard which constructed and repaired Super Aircraft Carriers, and also repaired Cruisers, Destroyers, and a variety of Navy vessels.

The New York Naval Shipyard, commonly called the Brooklyn Navy Yard, developed into the largest of the Navy's eleven shipyards and is among the world's largest. Its facilities cover 291 acres and include: 270 major buildings with more than six million square feet of floor space, 18 miles of paved roads, 9 piers, 24 miles of railroad tracks, 23,278 linear feet of crane tracks, and 16,945 feet of berthing space. The Yard had six modern dry docks, shops, warehouses, lumber yards, research laboratories. It had every type of industrial facility necessary for building, berthing, and servicing the most modern ships afloat. More than 98 different trades worked in the Yard's 22 shops. Shipyard employment reached a peak of 70,000 at the height of World War II. In 1953 the average was about 15,000. Many of the immortal ships of American Naval History, since 1801, were either built or serviced at New York Naval Shipyard.

The New York City Naval Shipyard

The Apprenticeship Program was a four year program, its mission to educate and train men to become proficient journeymen in a particular trade. This training did not limit an individual to a journeyman status. Training also provided the Navy Yard with future inspectors, planners, supervisors, instructors, and middle level managers. During the four year course of study, individuals would receive one week of classroom/shop instructions in the Apprenticeship School and four weeks of field experience. "The field" meant working at the outside dry docks and onboard ships, both old and new work. In school subjects were trade theory and performance, mathematics, physics, chemistry, drafting, blueprints, metallurgy, strength of materials, testing materials, technical writing, and elementary supervision. Each year the level of instruction became more advanced. Training was technical and practical. Practical field experience gave the individual not only knowledge and skills needed to perform his duties efficiently, but also the ability to work under the most adverse conditions imaginable. For instance a welder who worked in the dry docks onboard a ship, whether new construction or repair work, had to be able to work with a helmet, a face shield, heavy leather gloves, and a heavy leather jacket; be able to climb up a high scaffold or mast, or crawl into a tight confined space deep in the ship's holes to do a welding job. Welding utilizes intense heat to melt metal into a molten state which is manipulated to join together two different pieces of metal. The working conditions were far from ideal. In the summer temperatures below docks or below decks are stifling. For a welder, with all of his protective leather clothing, his creating molten metal causes the air to become unbreathable. Heat, smoke, and fumes cause many a man to pass out. In winter, if a welder is to work on a scaffold or a mast, the cold temperatures and wind across the river causes men to freeze no matter how much clothes he wears. An individual had to constantly be aware of his surroundings, as many got hurt badly or killed. One could easily fall off a scaffold or decking 20 stories high, or have something fall on him from above. The work in the Naval Yard, despite all of its safety programs, was always hazardous and dangerous. Insurance premiums, for those who wanted insurance, were rated higher for a shipyard worker than a miner, lineman, fireman or policeman.

Part of Apprentice training involved not only skills of the trade, but also the safety and survival of workers under these extreme conditions.

A unique feature of the Apprenticeship Program was the rotation of field experience. Every five weeks an apprentice was assigned or reassigned to a different area of the field. Sometimes within the same "Gang," and other times to a different Gang. There were 50 Gangs and 50 supervisors in the Welding Division and the rotation system gave an apprentice a variety of experiences. The system could also give an individual relief from a bad situation be it environmental or personalities. One unfortunate fact in being an apprentice was that he was always at the bottom of the pecking order. An apprentice always got the jobs that were unpleasant, jobs no mechanic (journeyman) wanted to do. Most apprentices who were not married did not last more than a year. Those who completed the four year program were usually married and had children. Whether it was maturity, responsibility, or whatever, the married men took all the dirt thrown at them. Especially veterans. They had no choice as the times were tough for a man without a trade. They had to graduate.

Domenick realized that he was not only

responsible for himself, but also for his wife and child — and possibly more children. He resigned himself to make the Navy Yard his career. In a way he was proud to work in the Yard, which was located in his area, an area rich in history. Many Revolutionary War battles were fought in and around his neighborhood. Streets and avenues were named after famous generals. Lafayette Avenue, Washington Street, Pulaski Street, Koskiosko Street, and Von Steuben Street. Domenick walked these streets hundreds of times. Fort Green Park, with its cannons and 10-story lookout tower, had many children playing on its hills, in and around its bushes. As a boy Domenick often relived the battles.

A surprise package was delivered to the Scarlato family by a very strong stork. The accepted Catholic rhythm system, which worked in the past, did not work now. Vickie became pregnant shortly after the birth of Toni. She was due to deliver in December of 1954. This made for an interesting story.

When Domenick was in the waiting room, waiting for Vickie to have the baby, he looked out a window and saw that it was snowing. It was a beautiful sight as the Brooklyn Hospital overlooked Fort Greene Park. The park was completely white. Domenick had a good feeling that everything would be all right, especially since it was December 22 and close to Christmas. Dr. Tortora, a young jovial doctor, came out of the delivery room and approached Domenick. He told Domenick to sit down.

"What's wrong? Is Vickie all right?"

The doctor said, "She is fine. Sit down."

Domenick sat.

The doctor said, "You have a set of twins."

"Quit kidding."

"Look, I am not smiling. You have twins."

Domenick blurted out, "What am I going to do with three babies?"

The doctor replied, "I don't know. You made them."

Dr. Tortora explained to the stunned father that he had twin girls. Now Domenick was not only stunned but dumbfounded that he had three girls. And Vickie at first would not believe that they had twins. Not until she held both of them, Linda and Diana, in her arms did she believe it. Both parents were totally confused because no one in the family on both sides had ever had twins, and these two babies were identical.

Vickie said to Domenick with tears in her eyes, "They are like triplets. All three in diapers…How are we going to do this?"

Domenick held back his own tears and answered, "Don't worry, we will manage nicely. We have two more beautiful healthy babies. I'm planning to make more room in the apartment and we have enough money saved to take care of our babies. I have a steady job as an Apprentice Welder at the Navy Yard…" (Although he would never admit that he hated it.)… "And we are all in good health, and working together we will make our home a happy one."

There were no hospitalization plans in those days.

Consequently people paid the doctor and hospital out of their own pockets. This medical bill was higher than normal and payment took all of Domenick's savings. This was devastating as his goal was to finish college as soon as possible and get his degree. It was a set-back, but he said, "Well I'll take a rest for a while and save some money for next year to go back to NYU...I hope."

Unfortunately this never happened as with the best of plans things never go as planned. Toni, their first-born girl, was eighteen months old when Linda and Diana were born. It was indeed like having triplets. Things were tight in the five room, coal water flat. Domenick had stayed in this coal water flat for two reasons. One, it was rent controlled. Two, more importantly, it was close to his job and New York University. Time was always at a premium so being close to work and school was important. All of these events caused Domenick and Vickie to be stuck here. The unexpected bundles of joy caused all, and then some, of the monies saved to be used to pay for the birth of the twins. The doctor was generous and only charged for one delivery. But the hospital charged double. Hopes for Domenick to return to NYU were gone.

Even though Domenick detested the working conditions at the Navy Yard, his performance was excellent. As noted the field experience was very practical and provided knowledge and skills. Apprentice Welders worked under the most adverse and dangerous conditions imaginable. Heat, sparks, and fumes were created by the electric arc. Extreme hot in the summer, freezing cold in the winter. Burns from the Electric Arc Welding and flame of cutting torches. The abuse an apprentice had to take were more than any human should endure. But endure a man must if he wanted to succeed. Domenick needed a steady income and he wanted to learn a trade. He knew if he could complete the four year course with above average grades, and get a good evaluation from the field, there would be opportunities ahead. He had plenty of motivating forces to keep from quitting.

But there was one time, in January 1955, when he almost quit his job. The birth of twins in December 1954 put a lot of pressure on Domenick, and this caused him to be tense and nervous. At work he tried his best not to allow things to bother him. One day in the dead of winter he was working on board an aircraft carrier. The carrier's flight deck was blanketed with a foot of snow and ice. Shipwrights had to clear the decks of the snow and ice so that welders could weld airplane cleats (tie downs) Even though these cleats were critical, second year apprentices were allowed to do the welds. It was freezing cold with the wind blowing across the river. A welder sat on an upside down bucket and the only movements were his hand and wrist, which were used to manipulate the molten metal. With his body relatively motionless he would start to freeze. The supervisor would have each welder relieved every two hours so he could warm himself inside the ship. Domenick had been welding for almost three hours and his toes were numb. His fingers began to hurt. He looked up at the Island of the flight deck. Inside, looking out from a porthole, were the Supervisor, a Quarterman, and a Chief Quarterman. There were over 1,200 men in the Welding Division and to see a Chief Quarterman looking down at him was very unusual. Though Domenick was freezing, the sight of a Chief Quarterman watching the welders work caused him to be nervous and he continued working.

Another hour passed and he "had it" so to speak. He again looked up at the Island and saw that the supervisor was alone and with a cup of coffee in his hand. Domenick "blew his top." He raced toward the island and threw his helmet with the attached face shield at the image in the porthole. Luckily the glass of a porthole is shatter proof. Domenick then steamed off the ship onto the dock. The Supervisor, whose name was Greenberg, ran after him and asked, "What's wrong?! What happened?!"

Domenick yelled at him. "You S.O.B. you relieved the Welders every two hours, but for me, a lowly apprentice, you kept me working for over four hours! I've had it. I'm quitting this chicken s*^t outfit!"

The Supervisor apologized and said, "You can't quit, you just had a set of twins. What are you going to do? How are you going to support a wife and babies?" He kept talking to Domenick trying to calm him down.

Domenick did finally cool down, and he remembered how much he needed this job. The Supervisor assured him that this would not happen again. He told him to take as long as he wanted to warm-up.

Domenick wondered. Did Greenberg actually have a heart? Or is he just afraid of what I would have told the personnel Office, including the Master of the Division, why he wanted to quit? It seemed like a good question.

It taught Domenick that there were times a man

must assert himself and not take too much crap. He wasn't in the military and civilians had rights. This lesson would help him in the future.

There were a number of incidents which were not pleasant during Domenick's apprenticeship. A few are worth mentioning. The first incident occurred during his second year as an apprentice. He was assigned to work on the Aircraft Carrier CVA-20 Bennington, which had been in a tragic explosion while operating at sea in 1954, an explosion which created many fires. Damage was most severe and the fires somehow spread through the ventilation system. The initial explosion occurred just below the Warrant Officers Ward Room, killing all of the Warrant officers as they ate lunch. Fire and smoke in the ventilation system burned and suffocated many sailors. The number of dead was 36. Many others were burned and badly hurt. The Bennington was brought into the Brooklyn Navy Yard for extensive repairs.

Domenick was teamed up with other Welder Mechanics and Shipfitters. He used a flame cutting torch to cut sections of twisted steel bulkheads and decks. He saw hair and skin stuck to some of the steel sections. It was a sickening sight Domenick would never forget. Worse still, some of his fellow workers cut through and into the Ward Room and found the mangled bodies of 20 Warrant officers. Domenick felt fortunate not to have witnessed that sight.

It took 3 months to get the Bennington operational again and able to rejoin the fleet. The cause of the explosion was never explained. This showed that even when ships are not in combat or in war, the dangers in their operations are always very much real. Serving and protecting the United States of America is a dangerous business. Domenick always said that the people must support, honor, and pray for servicemen.

"God Bless America and our troops!"

A second unpleasant incident happened when Domenick was working in one of the gigantic buildings in which giant pre-fabricated parts were assembled. These huge assemblies were then raised by powerful overhead cranes and put onto barges to be floated over to the dry dock. The behemoth cranes on the docks would then pick up the assemblies and place them accurately into the dry dock. Shipfitters and Welders would tie-in the prefabricated assemblies together — and create a ship.

It was getting close to lunchtime and there were two Shipfitters who needed a large steel section cut by a Burner (Flame Cutter). The Burner assigned to the job was Tiny, who Domenick knew well. Tiny received word that his mother had a heart attack and he was needed at home. The Supervisor told Tiny to "punch out" and go home. Tiny was disconnecting his equipment when the two Shipfitters asked him to make a small cut so they would not be "hung up." Tiny figured the small cut would only take a minute or two so he proceeded. What Tiny didn't know was that the powerful overhead crane was in the process of lifting a giant steel sheet of armor plating from its storage rack in a triangle configuration. Although Tiny and the Shipfitters were quite a distance from the storage rack, it still presented a serious problem if one of those steel sheets titled over. It is to be noted that when a crane is lifting any object the crane operator is required to blow a horn so that anyone in the area is alerted and can move away. This crane operator, about to lift the sheet of steel, did not blow his horn. As the crane lifted the plate, it tended to slide along the other plates in an upward path. This was normal. But in this case the bottom edge of the lifting plate caught on the top edge of another plate resting on the opposite side. This caused the opposite side plate to tilt over and come crashing down on Tiny. He was immediately cut in half. The two Shipfitters were standing just far enough away to be spared. The only thing that happened to the Shipfitters was that they were shook-up. Domenick, working on the other end of the building, heard and felt the tremendous crash of the massive plate. He does not want to describe what he saw, but it was another sight added to his nightmares.

During his apprenticeship, Domenick joined the Colombia Association, an Italian-American fraternal organization. Originally the organization formed to help its members when in dire need and also to promote social activities. There were over 900 members working in the Navy yard. As in any large organized group, no matter what kind, there is politics. Domenick attended some meetings and social events and eventually got involved in operations. He was voted in as the organization's secretary. Being very personable, smart, and efficient, he became popular not only among the Colombian members, but also with other organizations. But that is another story.

There were fifteen men in Domenick's Apprentice Welders complement. This group consisted of 13 White men and 3 Black men. It was said that Blacks had no opportunities. This was 1953 and Bill Wilkson, Waverly Hayman, and Bill Wheeler, all Black, made their own opportunities. They had received a good education, as they had to be in a high 90-percentile to get into the

Apprentices program. All were Korean War veterans, having served in the U. S. military. In fact most of the group were Korean War veterans, except for two WWII vets. The Korean War vets were George Ortega (Mexican-American) U.S. Army, Sy Silverman (Jewish-American) Navy, Harry Schols (German-American) Army, Dick Vollrath (German-American) Army, Orlando Fiorenza (Italian-American) Army, George Cohan (Irish/Italian-American) Navy, John O'Neil (Irish-American) Army, Eddie Claro (Italian-American) Army, Kenneth Hanson (Norwegian-American) Navy, The two WWII veterans were Hank Cespedes (Puerto Rican-American) U.S. Marine Corps, and Domenick Scarlato, Italian-American) U.S. Navy. This list points out the diversified ethnic or racial backgrounds. All were American in their hearts. Each man was independent and trying to make his own opportunity in his own way. This group of men not only worked closely together but became very tight as close friends can be. It is to be remembered that all of them were subjected to the same working conditions and training. It was like going through boot camp or basic training in the service. Fortunately they met every fifth week in the Apprentice School. There they exchanged work experiences, their military experiences, and their family and life experiences.

They became a close-knit working group. In fact, Domenick suggested they form a baseball team and compete against the established teams in the Navy Yard. Teams such as Shop 72 played against Shop 26, and so on. All the men thought it was a grand idea and they decided that Domenick should be their manager. Domenick agreed with one condition, which was that he be allowed to play. He scheduled the practice playoffs each Saturday at Taffee Place Park which had a large ball field. Since the ballpark was only around the corner from Domenick's home, he was able to easily schedule the field with the New York City Park Department.

Domenick being a generous and non-racial person used to invite the whole team to his house for lunch. Nobody ever refused his invitations. Vickie, being very generous and a tolerant person, welcomed each and every player. Even though the Scarlato family did not have much money, they always welcomed friends for lunches or dinner. Vickie was a genius in providing tasty meals. Besides playing baseball, these get-togethers were like a social club. Vickie enjoyed the men's company, especially the stories they told.

Wilkson, playing Center field, loved to jump and jive when he talked, and everything was, "Listen here, Jack." He was entertaining. Hyman, Left field, wore thick glasses, was very quiet, and appeared to be the studious type. Wheeler played Catcher, and always appeared to be nervous. He also appeared to doubt everyone's stories. Though most of the men were uneasy with Wheeler, they accepted him as one of their own. Ortega, Batboy, was short and husky with a wonderful sense of humor. If things got tense or depressed, they could count on Ortega to come up with a joke or two. Claro, playing Third base, was a terrific ball player but he had an attitude everything which was, "Don't worry about it." This saying would come back to haunt him in later days. Cespedes, Second base, was the oldest of the group. He was not only the most serious but also the most sensible. Hanson, Pitcher, had a very positive attitude. No matter what went wrong he always showed a brighter side. Fiorenza played First base. He was a pessimist and always looked at things on the dark side. He and Hanson were like oil and water, yet they were still good friends. Vollrath, in Right field, was a good hearted man, but with a superiority complex. He tended to look down on people. The group kept him in his place. Domenick played Short Stop, and was the organizer, manager, and morale booster for the team. He was a demanding person who knew how to get the most out of the men, while also keeping them happy. He was the glue that kept the group bonded together.

Each Saturday morning in the spring, the group diligently practiced. When the season opened up, Domenick had managed to get the Apprentice Team recognized by the Yard's "Baseball Commission." They played hard, but finished in last place. This did not damper their spirits as they all said like the Brooklyn Dodgers, "We'll be back next year." In the winter they still socialized when they were in Apprentice School, and sometimes with a drink or two at Flushing Avenue Sailor's bars. In fact, there was one time when Domenick's three Black friends suggested going to the Baby Grand Club on 125th Street and Lenox Avenue. Some of the men had reservations about going to Harlem. However Hank Cespedes, Eddie Claro, and Domenick sided with Bill Wilkson, Waverly Haman and Bill Wheeler. The six men went to the baby Grand Club in Harlem. They got a good table. No one bothered them. In fact they were treated warmly. They had a few drinks and listened to a good band and good singers. This was 1956 and they enjoyed a cheap, good, and entertaining night.

Domenick remarked to the group that there was a baby Grand Club in Brooklyn. It was located on Nostrand Avenue and Fulton Street in what was called Brooklyn's Harlem. He said he used to pass by the Club four nights a week when he attended Central Evening High School from 1948 to 1950. The high school was only two blocks from the baby Grand. No one ever bothered him. He had always wanted to walk into the Club but he never had time or money. Now he finally had the pleasure of going into the original baby Grand Club in Harlem. It was a good experience and a good show of comradery.

The next two years they played hard and they slowly moved up the ladder. In the fourth year, their graduating year, the Apprenticeship Team came in 2nd place. The team's picture appeared in the weekly newspaper, called the *Shipworker*, receiving their award. That was one proud day for the Apprentice team players. Vickie hosted a party for the team and their wives, with a large celebration cake and coffee. There were over twenty people in the Scarlato's apartment. Domenick's Aunt Angie thought everyone was nuts, but then again she had never saw a ballgame.

It is to be noted that 5 of the 15 apprentices did not play on the baseball team. George Cohan and Harry Scholz did not play because they lived in Long Island. Benjamin Simon was not interested in baseball. John O'Neil, who was single, quit the job after the first six months. Sy Silverman was fired exactly 20 days before his probationary period was to expire. As with all federal employees you must serve one year probation before becoming a permanent employee. All of the Welder Apprentices watched Silverman's progress. They used to say if he makes the year and becomes permanent then nobody would ever be fired.

Silverman was a colorful character and his story is worth telling. He was a single, carefree young man who was honorably discharged from the U. S. Navy. A free spirited soul. He didn't care to be bothered by any problems life could dish out. He was always late for work, took days off, never paid his mounting parking tickets for his beat-up convertible Chevy, and he spent money like it was water. He was loyal to his friends and very generous. If he had his last dollar in his pocket and a friend needed a dollar, he would give it to him. Silverman would dwell on a problem, no matter how serious, for about one minute and then say, "That's it, let's have some fun." When the apprentices attended classes at the Apprentice School, Silverman would fall asleep. When the English teacher would ask a question on technical English, he picked on Silverman. He would give the answer to the question as if read directly from a text book. If he was caught dozing in the field by the Supervisor, he would talk his way out of the situation by saying he had been praying. Silverman's downfall was his unauthorized absences, his tardiness, and his being investigated by a number of police agencies. The Navy department finally fired him. He was left with the New York City police trying to serve him with a warrant for his hundreds of parking tickets. The same police department was also looking to arrest him for living with a 15 year old girl, even though she looked 20 years old. Lastly, he was wanted by federal authorities for impersonating a sailor. The last word the apprentices heard about Silverman was that he was on a "tramp steamer" working as a cook. Yes, Silverman was a colorful character and each man in the group sort of admired him. They would always remember Silverman's face that looked like a boxer, though he was non-belligerent and a gentle person. It's unfortunate that his free spirit went wild, but he created a legend. He was like the main character from "Cool Hand Luke." Maybe the group all wished they could say, "The hell with it all" and take off and do as they pleased. But the reality of it all for them was that it's only a dream.

The year the Apprentice Team won the 2nd Place

Award was their graduating year. Each man was now a full-fledged Journeyman, Welder Combination Mechanic, able to weld any type of Welding Process under any conditions presented. They were now so special to the federal government and the Navy that there was a separate seniority list for them.

Approximately 1200 men made up the Welding Shop, the largest shop in the Navy Yard. It was called Shop 26. There were two seniority lists for good reason. The first list consisted of well-qualified men who specialized in only one process, such as Electric Arc Welding (650) men, Gas Welding (20 men), Heliarc TIG Welding (125 men), Aircromatic MIG Welding (25 men), Flame Cutting Burners (250 men), and Metalizers (5 men). The second list was the Welder Combination Mechanics (125 men), who could do all of the above Welding Processes and then some. They had the technical knowledge to analyze jobs. Plus their training enabled them, in the future, to possibly become a Supervisor, Inspector, an Instructor, a planner/estimator, or mid-management positions. The Navy Department made an investment in each apprentice, so if a "lay-off" occurred only the first list would be affected, never the second list. This was a good thing for the graduating class of apprentices. However, it must be remembered that it one stood as a Welder Combo Mechanic and never moved up the ladder, he would be like a Shock Trooper. There was no real permanent gang or place to work, but he could be sent wherever there was a need for immediate service. In other words, if the Electric Arc Welders are slowed up while waiting for possibly another trade to move in or whatever, they can hang around until needed. But the Welder Combination Mechanic would pack up his tool box and go to another job. For emergency jobs many times it was the Welder Combo Mechanic who got called in.

There were no real breaks. Still, the advantage of not being laid-off, having the technical knowledge to possibly move up the career ladder, were good motivations to stick around.

An incident which angered and depressed Domenick was Waverly Hayman's marriage. Hank Cespedes suggested to the group to have a stag party for Hayman. All agreed and were willing to contribute. Wilkson volunteered to have the party at his apartment. He lived in the Fort Greene projects as did Hayman. He said it would be easy to spring a surprise party on Hayman as he lived in the building next to him. Hayman frequently visited Wilkson so it wouldn't be unusual to have Wilkson call him over. Everyone in the group contributed money for beer, wine, and soda plus goodies. Each person brought a hot dish to the party and there was plenty to eat and drink. Wilkson provided the apartment, decorations, and music.

The surprise party was a success. Hayman was dumbfounded. As men would be men, they pushed and shoved and hugged Hayman. He was so happy he had tears in his eyes. Everything was going fine. Food, drinks, music, risqué jokes were super and each man was having a good time. Halfway through the party the people who lived on the same floor as Wilkson began to slowly drift into the apartment. Eventually there were a large number of people who really shouldn't have been there. Drinking got heavy and some people were more than just high. Comments were made by outsiders asking, what were the

"Whities" doing here. What surprised the group was that Wheeler, one of their own, was agreeing with them. Wheeler's attitude when he was drinking revealed his true feelings towards his White buddies. He was a racist.

Domenick knew that Blacks claim that only Whites are racist. This was far from the truth. Racism knows no color. Wheeler and Wilkson's neighbors were showing their true feelings.

These comments got worse and tensions began to rise. Hayman's friends had made the party and now they were being threatened with being thrown out. Wilkson tried hard to be the peace maker. Before matters could become violent, Domenick convinced his group to leave and finish their party at a neighborhood bar. They left the apartment and Fort Greene Projects and went down to Flushing Avenue Sailor's bar and had a good time.

This incident disturbed Domenick, as he was raised and schooled with Black friends. The only time he had trouble with Blacks was with the Flushing Avenue Gang, who were trying to horn in at Taffee Place Park. Gang wars were common in those days. In the Navy Domenick learned that the South was segregated and racist. The North, as far as he was concerned, took people for what they were worth. He didn't experience racism in his upbringing. He experienced discrimination and prejudices, but racism took on another dimension.

Hayman invited the entire group to his wedding. Domenick was reluctant to go as he felt this racial feeling among some Blacks would cause a fight or worse. He respectfully declined. Others of the group felt the same way. Three members went to the wedding, Hank Cespedes, Eddie Claro, and Kenneth Hanson. It is not necessary to describe their unpleasant experiences, but the abusive comments that the men and their wives endured was intolerant. To prevent any violence they left the reception hall. On Monday the three men described their experience. This infuriated Domenick, but he refused to allow it to influence his good relationship with his Black friends. This and other incidents made him more aware and sensitive to what was happening around him and in his country.

Also disturbing Domenick was that after graduation the tight group of friends were slowly drifting apart. They were scattered around the Yard. There were no more meetings at Apprentice School. Since they were no longer apprentices, the baseball team lost its legitimate standing as an Apprentice Team. Some of the players were absorbed by Shop 26 Team. Bill Wheeler and Kenneth Hanson went to play for Shop 26. That was the end of the Apprentice team.

Domenick stayed close with some of his classmates. George Ortega became his best friend and hunting and camping partner. Dick Vollrath, George Cohan, Bill Wilkson, and Waverly Hayman socialized occasionally. This was a disappointing and depressing time for Domenick, but he kept active by getting involved with a number of Navy Yard organizations. Hunting and skin diving were forms of therapy for him. Since Domenick had a large family and limited funds all his activities were done on a shoestring. If he went hunting for a deer he had to have a buddy who was compatible. Conditions were placed on the way they hunted, such as they only hunted on weekends, bringing pre-cooked food from home, using a surplus military rifle and cheap military ammo converted for hunting. It wasn't the best equipment nor most convenient, but Domenick did bring home a deer, which he shared equally with his hunting partner. Domenick's family was raised on deer, rabbit, and pheasant meat. Vickie was a good cook. All this helped the family budget.

As it was said, George Ortega, warmly called Georgie, became his best friend. Georgie was only 5-feet and 4-inches tall, stocky, and rather homely looking. His looks did not attract the opposite sex very well, but his personality was as beautiful as anyone could want. He was generous, loyal, and jovial, a true friend anyone could wish for. Georgie and Domenick were opposite in many ways, yet compatible. Georgie had one trait which was not only humorous but also made a bleak situation look bright.

They planned their first weekend camping trip to scout out an area for the coming deer hunting season. Both had limited funds so they equipped themselves with military surplus equipment. They shared the expenses equally when purchasing a military two-man Pup Tent, two used sleeping bags that could be zippered together, a kerosene lantern, two well-used Ski Trooper backpacks, two used ponchos, and a small Sterno stove the size of a Kellogg's Corn Flakes box. Vickie helped them plan their food menu including various cans of food. They were truly roughing it up.

At Domenick's home he and Georgie organized their equipment for the trip, most of this activity going on in the living room. Georgie swung the heavy ski trooper backpack around so he could put his arm through a shoulder strap. The pack was so heavy that the centrifugal force from swinging it around caused him to start spinning and he went flying onto the couch. This sight was so comical that Vickie, Domenick, and the children all started laughing. Both men began to figure out how to balance and reduce the weight of their packs.

A point to bring out about Georgie Ortega is that no matter how bad things got he always came up with some comical saying or act. When something wrong with anyone else, the time spent would be unpleasant or miserable for Domenick. No matter the situation with Georgie, Domenick got a good laugh, and the bad time became a good time.

At the crack of dawn they started their journey to the Catskill Mountains in Georgie's beautiful Mercury car. It was a bright sunny day and their spirits were high. They had just passed the George Washington Bridge when the car blew out a tire.

"This is a great start," Domenick remarked sarcastically.

Georgie replied, "It's not so bad. It could be raining."

With that it began to pour "Cats and Dogs." Domenick looked at Georgie who shrugged his shoulders, causing Domenick to smile. Both had a hardy laugh. In the rain they changed the tire. Upon putting on the spare tire they found that it needed air. Here they were with two flat tires. They had to walk and roll the tire off West Side Parkway to a gas station. Luckily there was a station open, and the attendant repaired the tire. Also both men chipped in and purchased another tire to replace the blown out tire. They waited for the attendant's associate to drive them back to Georgie's car. By this time it had stopped raining.

"Boy, were lucky it stopped raining," Georgie

stated.

Domenick stared at his friend. Then he grinned. They changed the tire and went on their merry way.

They finally arrived at a small town called Acra, which was probably not on any map. How they picked this area to explore state land is lost in time. This was their destination to climb this high mountain and map out an area to hunt. Huffing and puffing along an old logging trail, they found a suitable camp site, a flat patch of grass along a rapidly moving stream. They cleared the site, pitched the Pup tent, and arranged the area for some comfort. Georgie began cutting some firewood with a bayonet. He appeared to be having some trouble so Domenick went over to see if he could help. When he inspected the bayonet's blade he saw that it was not sharpened.

"Why didn't you sharpen this blade?" Domenick asked.

"I was afraid I might cut myself," was Georgie's answer.

"Next time we have to bring a hatchet."

When the campsite was set up, Daniel Boone and Chief Crazy Horse went scouting for deer tracks. Along various trails they noticed bear tracks.

"These are black bear tracks," Domenick informed his partner.

"Do they attack humans?"

"No, only if you bother them, or, if they are very hungry."

After locating a post near a possible deer path they went back to camp. On the way it began to rain. Domenick looked at Georgie, who smiled.

"We have been blessed!"

Thankfully it stopped raining at the camp site, but everything was wet. Georgie tried to start a cooking fire, difficult with wet wood. He kept trying and his small fire produced a lot of black smoke. He looked like a man billowing smoke. Domenick said that he was hungry and wasn't going to wait for a hot meal. He squatted in the Pup Tent and ate out of a cold can of beans. After what seemed like hours, Georgie got a good fire going and he ate a nice hot meal. His persistence paid off.

As the evening passed it began to rain hard. Both men retired to their sleeping bags. While lying quietly, Domenick noticed a small black spot on the tent's ceiling. He pointed out the black spot to Georgie. With that Georgie touched the spot to see what it might be. Little drops of water trickled down his finger. Soon the water slowly dripped onto the top of Domenick's head. He looked at his friend. As usual Georgie shrugged his shoulders and smiled. Domenick smiled back and turned around, with his head under his poncho, and went to sleep.

Later Georgie woke Domenick. "Do bears come into a camp?"

"It's possible, but unlikely at night."

Again Georgie woke Domenick. "What do we do

if a bear tries to get into the tent?"

"Shoot the bear in the head with your .22 rifle."

Georgie finally fell asleep with his rifle resting alongside of him.

In the morning the sun was shining brightly. Both men had a hot breakfast and then continued scouting the area. While resting on the trail, conversations usually were personal. They shared stories, especially about their boyhoods and even their relationships with their fathers. Domenick opened up his heart by revealing some of his experiences with his father. Georgie listened with great interest.

He began with the relationship between him and his father was always a strained one. Domenick always had to compromise to keep the peace. His father was an excitable person who could erupt in a moment, and cool down the next. He was easily upset, but his rage was short lived. When Domenick was born he had blue eyes like his father. His father was elated. Nine months later however, the child's eyes strangely changed to light brown like his mother's.

His mother told him later that his father cried when his eyes changed. This may seem like a small thing but it had an influence on the relationship. When Salvatore was born, his eyes were grayish blue so this made him the favorite son. For a number of years there were many incidents of favoritism towards Salvatore.

Normally this kind of behavior would cause jealousy between siblings, yet surprisingly Domenick overcame the tendency. As a boy and as a man he always protected and helped his younger brother. Domenick's father's attitude and behavior changed after he proved his worth by finishing evening high school in record time and then going to New York University. His multi-faceted talents were exceptional. Repairing his father's car and household items, and generally his knowledge in many areas. The trades, history, politics, or life in general. All of these factors caused his father to have a high regard for Domenick. Unfortunately, they also caused his father to become too dependent on him. Sadly his father had absolutely no talent for mechanical skills. He was always dependent upon others to fix things, paint, or do chores a man would normally do.

A number of times Domenick tried to get close to his father. He took him to the YMCA, and took him skeet shooting clay birds. Domenick even took him to the shooting range, and woodchuck hunting, and deer hunting. He spent as much time as he could with his dad, hoping to develop a rapport like he had with his grandfather. Sadly, it didn't work. He was always respectful of his father and helped him as much as possible, but they never could be close as Domenick wished it would be. Despite all their shortcomings Domenick loved his parents deeply. He was always there for them and the entire family.

Domenick wanted to look for another hunting

area, so he and Georgie planned a second camping trip to scout an area recommended to them by a Park Ranger. It was in the Catskill Mountains near Cairo, New York. They decided to go camping on Memorial Day weekend.

When Georgie and Domenick reached Cairo, the sky was clear, the sun was shining. They managed to locate the spot described by the Park Ranger. An old logging trail led them into State Park mountains. After an hour hike the road ended. The scenery was beautiful. They continued on, following an animal trail until they reached a roaring stream with a small waterfall. Here they pitched camp.

The rest of the day the two men walked the ridges. They spotted a farm below. Domenick spotted a woodchuck in the middle of a field. He said to Georgie that it is worthwhile to investigate because deer often graze in farm fields.

"That woodchuck might give us an opportunity for a shot at him."

They meandered to the edge of the field and found many fresh deer tracks. Domenick mentally noted this area for future consideration. The woodchuck popped up in the middle of the field. They were so far from the farmer's house that no one would hear the shot of a .22 rifle. The woodchuck couldn't see the two men because they were within the edge of the woods. Georgie told Domenick to "Indian up" on the woodchuck. With a .22 rifle he had to get close, real close, to the prey.

When Domenick was almost within range a frightening but comical thing happened. Out of nowhere came a bunch of cows and a bull. Domenick froze. The bull began slowly walking towards him, sniffing the air and the ground. It was definitely a bull, not a cow. It had a ring in its nose. Domenick pointed the .22 towards the bull's head, thinking. *I must be kidding but if it charges I've got to do something.* Meanwhile he could hear Georgie yelling, "Don't move!" As if Domenick didn't already know that. The bull stops and stares in Domenick's direction. He is close. Too close for comfort. *Why doesn't Georgie do something to distract this bull?"* Georgie must have read his mind because he came out from the woodline and partially into the field. He began waving his jacket. He also started yelling. "Arriba El Toro! Arriba!" Through the corner of his eye Domenick could see Georgie jumping around like a matador waving his jacket. Domenick could not help chuckling. The bull was distracted, away from Domenick and towards Georgie. The bull charged towards Georgie, who ran back into the woods. The bull didn't follow. All of this gave Domenick time to run for the woods. When both men got together again they laughed loudly and hugged each other. Domenick decided to forget this area for hunting. The men went back to camp, packed their gear, and headed home.

It had been an interesting weekend, with a new area discovered and plenty of stories to tell. Georgie and Domenick hunted together many times. They camped in other areas and each time improved on their equipment. They shared equally in everything, including whenever Domenick got a deer. He gave half to Georgie and his family. Finally they bought a good Eastwing hatchet, which Domenick still has today. Gone were the days of using a bayonet to chop wood for campfires. When they camped, Georgie made sure he had a big gun with him. Though they hunted in other areas of the state, they always favored the mountains around Cairo.

Domenick and Georgie were very close friends. He ate many a meal at Domenick's home. Vickie and the children were very fond of Georgie. When Georgie called on the telephone for Domenick and he wasn't home, Vickie could talk to him for hours. That was Georgie. He could talk and keep things interesting. Likewise, Georgie's family, his mother, father, sister, and two nieces, was fond of Domenick. Georgie wasn't married. He was devoted to his family. Every Saturday he took his mother and sister shopping.

It is a shame that Georgie was cut short in his early years. He passed away at the age of thirty-three. He died in his sleep. The family was so devastated that Maria, his sister, called Domenick at work to come and help them. Domenick and Vickie helped the family with funeral arrangements. Such a great loss for everyone. Whenever Domenick goes into his garage and sees that Eastwing hatchet hanging on his tool wall, he reflects back to the many times he and Georgie hunted together. Especially their first camping trip. Domenick would never part with the precious Eastwing hatchet.

To further the Scarlato's budget Domenick joined the Army National Guard in 1956. Hank Cespedes told him how he could make extra money in the Guard, and that he could easily attain the rank of Staff Sergeant. The National Guardsmen were called "Weekend Warriors" because they drilled one weekend per month and trained two weeks per year. Domenick joined Cespedes' outfit, the 773rd Anti-Aircraft Battalion. This battalion protected New York City with Nike missiles. Domenick was given the rank of Staff Sergeant. He and his men, along with

Army personnel, inspected missile sites throughout NYC and the Metropolitan Area. The weekend drills were held in the uptown Manhattan National Guard Armory, located on Amsterdam Avenue and 69th Street. Two-week training sessions were performed at Camp Drum, Watertown, New York. Training was extreme and effective. Between the regular U.S. Navy, the Naval Air Reserve, and the Army National Guard, Domenick had almost ten years of service. If he had re-enlisted and stayed in the Guard for another ten years he could have received a small pension for the rest of his life. *Why didn't Domenick re-enlist?*

In 1959 almost all of the guardsmen were veterans of WWII and/or the Korean War. During this time many men were joining the Guard to avoid the Draft. Among the many joining were Puerto Ricans. It is unfortunate that most of the Puerto Ricans did not, or pretended not to, speak or understand English. Hank Cespedes was Puerto Rican-American and a WWII veteran. It annoyed him that he had to speak Spanish to his men who made no effort to learn English.

There was an incident in which Domenick almost got into trouble because of a language barrier. He had given a simple order to one of his men who did not respond. Domenick attempted in a number of ways to convey this order, and he felt the man was playing games with him. Out of frustration, Domenick picked up the man by his collar and was shaking him when an officer yelled out, "Sergeant, put that man down! We do not do this in today's Army!" This convinced Domenick that the Guard had a real problem. This lack of communication hindered the training and effectiveness of the outfit. Veterans said the outfit was being weakened, and if it were federalized and sent overseas to combat, they would be wiped out. With this kind of attitude permeating throughout the outfit, many veterans chose not to re-enlist. Domenick, with regrets, did not re-enlist in the Army National Guard.

Domenick not re-enlisting in the National Guard was not only a loss of time towards a military pension but also a loss of extra money for the family. Money was hard to come by, as it was needed for daily living expenses and high medical bills. There were no healthcare programs available at that time. Medical bills were paid in cash.

At the age of five Toni almost died from a severe asthma attack. She was hospitalized, given oxygen and extensive medical care. Batteries of tests resulted in the need for special injections to be given religiously each week. This treatment went on for over ten years.

Linda and Diana both needed monthly injections for allergies. Also Linda suffered a severe concussion from being hit in the head by an adult swing. She was hospitalized and required later treatments. Twin sister, Diana, experienced a smashed knee from falling off a high-flying adult swing.

Vickie's chronic bouts of Phlebitis in her legs caused her to be incapacitated for two or three weeks on a number of occasions.

The cost of medical treatments for chronic health problems, plus the normal medical and dental bills, kept the Scarlato family from being able to get ahead. Domenick constantly looked for overtime on his job, and he worked part-time at home doing gunsmith work.

On December 2, 1958, Domenick looked up at the sky and saw a streaking Comet plummeting towards the earth. This reminded him of when he was ten years old and had watched a white streak falling to earth. That sight scared him to no end. He thought it was a ghost or spirit and he ran home as fast as he could run. He told his mother what he had seen. She told him that it was not a ghost but only a Comet. Domenick thought this December 2, 1958 Comet must be a good vision because on this day his fourth child was born. Barbara was healthy and beautiful with a shocking head of curly hair. She looked three months old.

With Toni, Vickie and Domenick were able to enjoy raising one baby. When the twins were born it became purely frustrating work. The changing of diapers, three babies, 6 to 8 times a day kept the washing machine going all day. The long clothesline, 3 stories up, was constantly filled with clothes, especially diapers. Vickie said, "God Bless the Norge washing machine for lasting two years before it broke down." Domenick was regularly repairing this much needed appliance. Multiple feedings, washing, waking in the middle of nights with three babies was exhausting. One baby would cry and wake up the other two babies. Both Vickie and Domenick walked the floor with each baby to calm them down. Also they both said thank God for Aunt Angie and Uncle Frank living in the apartment below them. Their help at times during the day was invaluable, as they were like a grandmother and grandfather to the children. It took a couple of years before the young parents could experience the real joy of having three kids in the house. It took time to realize that the twins were a blessing.

Domenick tried his best to treat each child equally. This was not easy. When Barbara was born the other children were five years-plus old. Being the new baby,

Barbara of course required more attention than her older sisters. Sometimes this was misconstrued as showing favoritism, which tended to spoil her. Possibly all of this special attention to the small baby, and later as the youngest child, there may have truly been favoritism. Nonetheless, Vickie and Domenick did indeed try to be fair with each child,

For example, the parents had to make sure at suppertime that each dish and each glass contained an equal amount of ingredients for each child. Another example was birthdays. The child with the birthday received a gift, but the other children also got a small gift. As they got older and were more understanding these practices were slowly changed.

When Domenick had been a journeyman for two years, he saw an announcement for a Supervisor's competitive examination. He always remembered what his grandfather Domenico had said. "Each generation must do better than the last generation." Without hesitation he filed for the exam. He was very successful in passing the written examination with a 100%. This gave him 50% towards his final grade. His personnel folder gained him the complete allowable total of 25%, and the personal interview by a Supervisor, Quarterman, and the Master of the Shop gave him 20%. His final grade was 95%. In 1960 he was appointed to a supervisory position.

He served a trial period for six months between the Sheetmetal Shop 17, the Pipe Shop 56, and the Shipfitters Shop 11. He was then given charge of a 20-man Gang working aboard the Supercarrier CVA-62 Independence. Domenick worked diligently to make sure each man was treated humanely. He distributed work orders fairly. His primary concern was for the safety of men, and he personally made sure that each assignment given had a safe working environment. Although Domenick was fairly new as a Supervisor, he gained the respect of his men and the respect of other trades. His excellent work in the next two years did not go unnoticed. The Master of Shop 26, Mr. Stuchell, was very much aware of his performance. Domenick's ability to get the most out of his men and stay ahead of scheduled production dates was a big plus for his evaluations. His technical knowledge was above average. When a problem arose which slowed or stopped work, Domenick always came forth to help solve the problem. A beneficial Suggestion Program existed, in which any Shipworker could participate by making a suggestion. If a suggestion saved the government money, the worker would get either a certificate or money. The amount of money depended on how much the government would save. Domenick made numerous suggestions which were adopted effectively. All were recorded in his personnel folder. All these attribute earned Domenick excellent reports and evaluations. When an Instructor of Apprentices position opened up, Mr. Stuchell called Domenick into his office for a personal interview. He first asked if Domenick if he would be interested in the position, as he had the authority appoint an Instructor. Domenick almost fell off his chair, but without hesitation he answered, "Yes, and I will do an excellent job." This is exactly what the Master of Shop 26 wanted to hear. Domenick did not know that the Master had already interviewed six other supervisors, none of whom were acceptable. Domenick's work performance, his personnel folder, his educational background, and his personality made him the prime candidate. In1962 he was appointed Instructor of Apprentices.

As an Instructor of Welder Apprentices, Domenick was assigned to the Apprentice School in what was called Building No. 5. His job was to teach Welding Technology, Strength of Materials, trade Mathematics, Blueprint Reading, and Safety Procedures. Building No. 5 housed all of the Apprentices from over twenty-two trades, with fourteen full-time Instructors and eight part-time Instructors. Additionally there were three non-trade Instructors, for English, Physics, and Mathematics. Domenick did not realize that he had been appointed to be a part-time Instructor. He was required to teach a half day at the school and then supervise a half day at the Sheetmetal Shop. This was a tricky situation with numerous problems. Still, he accepted without reservations. He rationalized that this was a start and it would keep him out of the harsh elements of the dry docks.

Mr. Cozzie, Apprentice program Administrator, for whatever reason did not care for Shop 26 and its Welding Apprentices. This fact wasn't told to Domenick and it hindered his teaching efforts. He had no desk nor a file cabinet in the Instructor's Room. When he requested typing service or reproductions of educational information sheets, Mr. Cozzie would stonewall. Whenever Domenick spoke to him he never smiled. He appeared to be a grumpy old man. Domenick was frustrated but he overcame his obstacles. He did his lesson plans at home. His wife, Vickie, typed all his information sheets. Through pure personality he charmed a secretary named Nancy to reproduce them. Nancy and Domenick became good friends. She helped him in many ways to adjust, especially to the Mr. Cozzie problem. Many times she would give him extra paper, chalk, or stationery items. She even helped him order training films from the Navy library. One time to show his appreciation he took Nancy to lunch. Unfortunately, Nancy had developed a crush on him, and so this lunch only made her want to get closer. She was a beautiful single girl with brown hair and green eyes. This situation could have developed into an affair more than simply friendship. Domenick being married and true blue to his wife did not permit this friendship to go any further.

Domenick researched over and above what was required to teach his apprentices. He joined the Welding Engineering Society and received their Welding Journal, which had many technical articles on the latest welding technology and techniques. He went to Society meetings of local professionals. He went to Welding Conventions and Fairs in order to talk to manufacturers and vendors about the latest equipment. Domenick always came back with a huge amount of pamphlets, books, and other literature for his apprentices. Many Welding Supervisors throughout the Yard heard about Domenick's extra activities. They asked him for his educational sheets, which he had developed on his own. After about nine months, Mr. Stuchell heard about Domenick's work and he scheduled an appointment to talk to him. They did meet and talked, and Mr. Stuchell saw the advanced work he was doing on his own initiative. He also saw the difficulties Domenick was having as a part-time Instructor. Mr. Stuchell told Domenick that he would appoint him as a full-time Instructor. He also stated that he was proud of the work he was doing and complimented him for bringing pride to the welding shop. Mr. Stuchell called the Superintendent of the Apprentice School, Mr. Longstreet, and related Domenick's situation. Mr. Longstreet said he would take care of the problem. Before the end of the week Domenick was provided with a desk plus a file cabinet in the

Instructor's Room. Any clerical work he requested would be immediately provided by the secretaries.

Mr. Cozzie was steaming, but he had to take this with a smile. Domenick never took advantage of his connection with Mr. Stuchell. He simply continued to do over and above what was asked of him.

As a full-time instructor, Domenick came under the direct supervision of the Apprentice program Administrator. Mr. Cozzie asked him if he could fill in for one of the instructors to do a Job Orientation Session. Domenick rarely ever said no to an assignment.

"How long is an Orientation Session and what do I do with my classes?"

Mr. Cozzie replied, "The Session takes about three hours. Your classes can be doubled up with other classes, such as blueprint reading and mathematics."

Domenick accepted the assignment and was given a large informational book to study. The Job Orientation Session was a lecture which orientated new employees, such as engineers, laborers, office workers, mechanics, management, etc. Its purpose was to help them adjust to their new government jobs. This was a big nut to crack and Domenick had only a weekend to study the large book and prepare to give a three hour lecture on the history of the Navy Yard, the Yard's mission, the multiple benefits offered by the government. He had to address the location of various shops, cafeterias, medical facilities, police, firemen, and then answer a myriad of questions at the end of the session.

On Monday morning Domenick was prepared. There were approximately sixty people in the auditorium. And lo and behold, sitting in the back of the auditorium was Mr. Cozzie and Mr. Longstreet. This looked very suspicious to Domenick. Was he being set up for a fall? No matter. He had worked hard all weekend preparing and was determined to do well. He made sure his lecture would not be boring. First, he made the Navy Yard's history come alive. Information given was factual with some added humor. His question and answer session was thorough and accurate.

After about forty-five minutes, Mr. Longstreet and Mr. Cozzie left the auditorium, only to return periodically to listen in. This disturbed Domenick but he refused to let it rattle him. He continued lecturing as though nothing bothered him. Later that day, Mr. Longstreet called Domenick to his office. When he arrived, who was sitting beside the Superintendent but Mr. Cozzie. Domenick was nervous. Could he have been so bad as to be called to this office?

Well, on the contrary, Mr. Longstreet complimented Domenick on a job well done. He offered Domenick a permanent place with the Orientation Team. The Team not only orientated new employees, but also went to various city high schools to lecture graduating seniors about the Navy Yard's Apprenticeship Program. They also acted as Proctors in administering the Apprentice Competitive Examination. Domenick was flattered and of course accepted. Because this assignment was in addition to his teaching duties it had to be approved by Mr. Stuchell, Master of Shop26. Without reservation, Mr. Stuchell approved Mr. Longstreet's recommendations.

Mr. Cozzie was suddenly Domenick's buddy. He couldn't do enough for him. Again, Domenick did not take advantage of this new friendship, as he did not want to lose his good working relationship with other

instructors. [Figure 7 & 8]

Figure 7: Navy Yard Apprenticeship Program;

Instructor Domenick Scarlato center

What I Got From My Apprenticeship"

EDITOR'S NOTE: After four years as an apprentice, Theodore Rose of Shop 26 is about to complete his training and step into the mechanic ranks. As part of the classroom phase of his training he was asked to write an essay on the subject "What I Got From My Apprenticeship." Following is his impressions just as he wrote them. We are printing them because we feel Mr. Rose's words eloquently describe our Apprentice Program in a manner no professional writer could equal. And by so doing, he makes himself a symbol of the high calibre of ALL of our apprentice graduates.

"In September 1958 I started working at the Shipyard as an apprentice welder. At that time I had no conception of the magnitude, hence, the tremendous variety, of jobs that are performed here.

"Through the indoctrination class I soon became familiar with the history of the Shipyard and more important, I was given vital information on the things I could expect and what was expected of me as a civilian employee of the Navy.

"For a new apprentice entering into the everyday activities of shipyard work, there is a never ending amazement at the tasks that are being accomplished. It did not take me long to realize that a great deal of concentration and effort on my part was to be required if I wished to adapt myself to the stringent requirements of the shipyard.

"My instructions in the subjects and principles pertaining to the different methods of welding was, to say the least, most interesting experience, especially since the whole field of welding was something I had ever given much thought to as it was becoming a trade, hence livelihood.

"Working in the Shipyard

Going over test papers with Theodore Rose (right) are apprentice instructors Ernest Dimitry (left) and Dominic Scarlato.

side by side with mechanics who possess various degrees of skill and experience in my particular trade, I have gotten a better general understanding of the principles and theory behind different welding combinations and methods that are employed in

welding various types of metals.

"The academic training and overall general information that I have received in the Apprentice Program have been a great help to me as far as understanding the relationship of my trade to the overall mission of the Shipyard."

Also calling on Adm. Holzworth last Friday were Rep. Paul A. Fino of the Bronx (holding papers), and State Assemblyman Luigi R. Marano of Brooklyn (third from right). Joining in the meeting were Columbia Association officers, Grand Master Daniel Stea of the Service Trades, and James Dolan, Metal Trades Council President. Rep. Fino and Assemblyman Marano also toured the Shipyard and came away greatly impressed by the extensive shipbuilding and repair facilities. Left to right are: Domenick Scarlato, Anthony Chimenti, Mr. Stea, John Giannone, Mr. Dolan, Alex Di Clemente, Adm. Holzworth, Columbia President Rocco Emancipator, Rep. Fino, Assemblyman Marano Joseph Baili and Frank Puglisi.

Figure 8: Admiral Holzworth center; Domenick far left

As previously mentioned, Domenick was actively involved with the Catholic Men's League and the Columbia Association. He served as Secretary for both worthwhile organizations which provided benevolent help to their members in need. He made many friends. He participated in many activities such as charity drives, blood drives, dances and other social events. In fact he received so many notices in the Navy Yard's newspaper, *Shipworker*, that the National Association of Government Employees Union approached him and asked him to run for the National Secretary position. It is to be noted that the Catholic Men's League had 1,200 members, the Columbia Association 900 members, and the N.A.G.E. Union had over 4,000 members. To hold the position of Secretary with all three organizations would be a daunting challenge, but Domenick knew he could do it. He could not accept the challenge without first consulting with Vickie. They talked in great length. She knew he had a tremendous amount of energy and needed such outlets. The hunting, scuba diving, and YMCA activities satisfied him physically, but Domenick needed something to exercise his mind and spirit. She agreed to support him 100%

Domenick campaigned for the N.A.G.E. Secretary position. To make a long story short, he won easily. His reputation, personality, exceptional speeches and effort helped him win in a landslide. He was efficient and effective. He became popular with members of all three organizations. All three enabled him to meet with many middle and upper management groups.

These meetings gave Domenick a good deal of positive exposure and valuable experiences. [See Figures #9 & #10]

Figure 9: Columbia Assoc. officials installed

Figure10: Columbia Association officials

In the spring of 1961, Domenick experienced a tragic event involving the U.S.S. CVA-64 Constellation. The third Super Carrier being built in the Brooklyn Navy Yard caught fire. She was about 90% completed when a fire broke out on the Hanger Deck, which spread because of a ruptured large Aviation test Tank. The fire covered the entire hanger Deck, burning everything in its path, scaffolding, staging, etc. Since this was "new construction" there were no Navy Sailors aboard to man fire watches. Consequently the blaze was out of control within minutes.

The high winds from the river, the wood staging, the aviation fuel, etc. burned so intense that when one looked at the ship from a distance the two Hanger Doorway openings—at least 20 feet high and 100 feet wide—looked like blast furnaces. It was later found that the temperature of the fire had to be over 1500° as the 5" armor deck of the hanger deck was warped so badly it looked like a 1/4mile roller coaster.

There were two companies of Navy Yard firefighters plus firefighters from Brooklyn, Queens, Manhattan, and from Jersey City and Newark. The fire burned for over 24 hours and there was so much water pumped onto and into the carrier that she started to list at least 18° away from the dock.

Six hundred civilian tradesmen were working aboard the Constellation when the fire erupted. All of the men working on the Hanger Deck were killed. Others tried frantically to escape the flames. Men on the Flight Deck were being lifted by the cranes to the dock. Many men simply jumped into the river. A large number of workers were trapped below the Hangar Deck with no way to escape.

The Navy Yard P.A. System broadcast a constant

plea for volunteers, especially Burners (Welders) to come to the aid of the trapped men. What was needed were men to cut holes in the side of the ship in order to free the men trapped inside. This was a very dangerous assignment.

Domenick was an instructor at Apprentice School when he heard the pleas for help. He went to the Apprentice Program Administrator and he said,

"I'm leaving my class and I am going down to the dock to help in any way I can to get those men out."

Six welders (Burners) and Domenick were loaded onto a barge with flame-cutting equipment. They were floated over to the listing side of the ship. Wherever they heard trapped men banging inside, they would cut holes in the side of the ship.

As they cut these large holes, smoke would billow out and trapped men would spill out. Some men were hurt, some suffering from smoke inhalation, and some simply exhausted. The barge had to be moved many times and they had to work fast, as there was a possibility of the Carrier capsizing on top of them. [Figure 11]

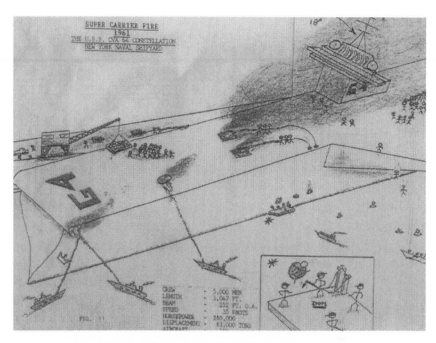

Figure 11: CVA-64 Constellation fire 1961

The sound of men screaming desperately for help while hanging onto bulkheads will always ring in Domenick's ears. To see coughing men spill out of the just cut holes was a good sight. But seeing burnt bodies pulled outside was too much for any man to bear.

Many men were saved. The actual number Domenick cannot remember. After more than twenty-four hours the fire was finally put out, and the carrier was saved. Hundreds of pumps worked to pump out the water to get the Constellation upright. It took a year and a half to finally complete and commission U.S.S. CVA-64 Constellation, so she could join the fleet.

There were over three hundred men burned, injured, or smoked by the tragic fire. Fifty-five men were killed. Five of the dead were Welders, all of whom Domenick knew very well. The fifty-five bodies were placed in Bldg. 294. The next day he visited the building and witnessed the deceased bodies, which were placed in rows and covered with canvas covers. This memory, as with other tragic memories, will burn in his mind forever.

Seven Welders/Burners, six Shipfitters, six Riggers, and four Barge Handlers (including the crew of the Tug Boat) received the Admiral Holtzworth Commendation Medal.

Another tragic but exciting incident that Domenick was involved with was the Cuban Missile Crisis of 1962. In October of '62 the Russians placed missiles in Cuba, which threatened the United States and the Western Hemisphere. This move by Russia and Communist Cuba created tremendous pressure for the U.S. to act. President

John F. Kennedy stated that any missile launched from Cuba to any country would be an act of war against the United States, and that we would retaliate by attacking Cuba and Russia. The President gave an ultimatum to Russia to remove those missiles from Cuba. The Russians did remove their missiles from Cuba. This avoided a WWIII confrontation.

During this crisis our entire military was on alert and we had our base at Guantanamo, Cuba on full alert. Our Sailors and Marines at Gitmo were fully armed and all roads and areas around the base were mined. Fidel Castro cutoff the freshwater supply to our Gitmo base, but our Navy had special evaporators to turn seawater into freshwater; consequently this did not affect our servicemen. Also during this time our Navy was patrolling the waters off Cuba. One of our aircraft carriers, CVQA-64 Constellation, was experiencing trouble. One of the catapults which launched jet aircraft was malfunctioning. The carrier already was patrolling the Cuban waters and could not be taken off the line for repairs.

Since this Super Carrier had been built in the New York Navy Yard (Brooklyn), the Navy requested a team of civilian Navy Yard workers who were experienced in carrier work. The Team consisted of 6 Pipefitters, 2 Welder Combo Mechanics, Instructors, and a Supervisor. This team was to be flown aboard the carrier and correct any problems the ship may be experiencing.

Domenick and another Welder, John Brady, were selected for the Team by Mr. Stuchell, master of Shop 26. The Team flew from Floyd Bennet Field, New York, to the Naval Airfield in Norfolk, VA, and then onto the CVA-64 Constellation. While they circled the carrier in a holding pattern, they observed a plane catapulted from the carrier and it crashed into the sea. It was a horrific sight. Now a second catapult was having trouble. Their plane was held in a holding pattern for close to an hour before being waved off to go to Guantanamo Naval Airfield. During the time they spent in the holding pattern circling, destroyers were close by, but it was the helicopters that executed the rescue. They could observe that there were sharks in the water, but none were menacing the downed airmen. They later learned that of the three airmen in the water, one had died and two were badly injured.

They landed at Gitmo and were billeted at the B.O.Q. (Bachelor Officer's Quarters). They were all treated as officers — they slept, ate, and mingled with the officers. They even used the Officers' Club. After two days in Gitmo they finally took a flight and landed on the CVA-64 Constellation. This experience brought back memories when in 1951 Domenick was in the Naval Air Reserve and made carrier landings onto the U.S.S. CVA-41 Midway while serving as a gunner on a TBM Avenger.

Aboard the constellation the team worked twenty-four hours a day with minimal breaks as the aircraft carrier continued underway and patrolled Cuban waters. They worked in 120° to 130°F temperatures while welding, cutting, etc. in the hole of the catapults. Brady and Domenick took half-hour turns welding structures, piping, etc. After ten days both men had lost over twenty pounds. There were times when pipefitters, and Brady, passed out. Domenick got dizzy numerous times but didn't pass out. The team completed its mission in less than two weeks. Both catapults were made fully operational. The men were flown off the carrier and back to Gitmo for a two-day rest and lay over.

As Domenick relaxed at Gitmo, he reflected back to the spring of 1961 when this same carrier had suffered the worst fire at the Brooklyn Navy yard in Navy history. Domenick and others had cut holes in the side of the ship in order to free men trapped inside — and recover bodies. Many said that the Constellation was a jinxed ship — a "Jonas Ship." She did have many accidents and bad luck. Maybe, just maybe, there was some truth to Old Sailors' Superstitions about a Jonas Ship.

On February 3, 1962, Darlene Scarlato was born a healthy baby with blonde hair. She was a jovial chubby baby who ate and slept as most babies do. She was a blessing and did not show a temper at an early age. Having five daughters and living in a four room coal water flat was not an ideal setting, but Domenick and Vickie provided a loving environment and made sure their children were never deprived. It is to be noted that Domenick tore down one wall in their five room apartment to create more space for the children, making it a four room home. The play area was greater. Domenick said he felt like a Space Engineer as he was always making more space for his girls. Their home was always kept clean, pleasant and loving. They ate healthy foods and wore good stylish clothes. Medical needs, which were many, were maintained. The girls always had an area in which to play with their many toys. Vickie and Domenick had to go without many pleasures, and sometimes necessities, to provide family traditions, medical attention, Christian values and morals, a good education, patriotism, and the skills to become independent. Most important to them was to encourage loyalty and love for family and country.

Webster's Dictionary defines the word "Passion" with many words or phrases. The following words are chosen to describe Domenick's passions. His strong deep interest and desire for an object or subject, his enthusiasm, his zeal, and his intense emotion which compels action sums up Domenick's passion.

Domenick had many interests throughout his life but certain experiences would always remain with him. These were, to ride a horse, ride a motorcycle, fly in an airplane, hunt, workout in a gym, and swimming. Of these activities the one he continued most was swimming.

Domenick loved to swim. He learned at an early age. When he was twelve years old he learned to swim in the East River. Currents of the East River could at times be unpredictable, and he never forgot a time when a young boy drowned in that river. Domenick learned how to negotiate those currents. He traveled to many a place to swim, including Brooklyn Tech High School's pool and the Red Hook pool. In fact to get to the Red Hook pool he had to hitch on the back of a trolley and travel eight miles. There he and other kids would "sneak in" by climbing a very high fence. He swam on Coney Island beyond the jetties, and he even swam in the Rockaways in its high rough seas.

Domenick tried to teach his younger brother, Salvatore, to swim, but it wasn't until Salvatore was about ten years old that he really began to swim. They went to the Red Hook pool and it was there that Salvatore learned to swim well. In fact, Domenick had him diving off the diving board, even the twelve foot diving board. Domenick was there every step of the way to make sure he didn't get hurt. He loved and protected his younger brother. Domenick so excelled in swimming that he served in the U.S. Navy as a frogman in the Underwater Demolition Team—now known as the SEALs. In the 1960's Domenick qualified as an Instructor to teach S.C.U.B.A. diving at the YMCA. He also organized a Scuba diving club called the Aqua Knights Diving Club, and was its first president. Domenick taught scuba diving to members. The first members were his brother Salvatore (Treasurer), his brother-in-law, Dennis Dempsey, Cono "Sonny" Porcaro, Johnny Savino (Secretary), John Carrano (Vice President), and Anthony Ferro. The club grew to fifteen members, yet they kept the number small in order to create a closely knit group. Members had to look out for each other's welfare and safety. Most members were military veterans who understood the *Esprit de Corps*. [Figure 12]

Figure 12: Aqua Knights Emblem 1961

The first members of the Aqua Knights Diving Club were each unique in their experiences, but the veterans knew the meaning of comradeship. Salvatore was a Draftsman by vocation and had joined the U.S. Navy Air Corps at age seventeen. Feeling he needed something different, he had resigned from the Navy and was allowed to join the Marine Corps with his friends. As a Marine, he served honorably in Korea. One of his main passions was he loved to gamble.

Sonny Porcaro was a carpenter but he could fix anything. He had joined the Marines with Salvatore and also served in Korea. He was a true friend.

Anthony Ferro was also a carpenter who had served in the U.S. Army as a paratrooper during the Korean War. He was a kidder who loved to clown around. Still, he remained dead serious on a dive.

John Carrano was a Welder Combination Mechanic with the New York City Sanitation department. He was the oldest man in the club, but only by one year ahead of Domenick. He had served as an Aerial gunner on a B-17 Flying Fortress Bomber during WWII. A pessimistic type of guy, Johnny always looked for the worst that could happen, even if the sun was shining brightly. This could have been a consequence of the War, but it didn't affect his diving ability. Whenever he worried about "What if" the boat broke down, or something else, the guys would make jokes. Johnny laughed along with them. He was a dependable and loyal friend.

Johnny Savino, a truck driver for the Cascade Laundry Company, had joined the Marine Corps with Salvatore and Sonny. Luckily he had been assigned as a Fleet Marine aboard a Navy Heavy Cruiser. On a ship a Fleet Marine guards the Officers' Quarters and operates the brig. Johnny was overweight. He was 260lbs but that did not seem to hinder his ability to scuba dive. He had to constantly alter his wet suit in order to fit into it. He loved to eat.

Dennis "Dee" Dempsey, a truck driver for Dugan's Bakery Company, was 6'3" tall and very skinny. He had a slight speech impediment but participating in the Club helped him get rid of his stuttering. Through activities at the YMCA, Domenick helped Dee build up physically. Although Dee wasn't a veteran of the military he did try to fit in with the group.

All club members were required to join the Bedford YMCA. When Domenick taught scuba diving techniques, with attention to strict diving safety rules, he also stressed physical fitness plus comradeship and team work. Body building, basketball, and handball made being a "Y" member fun. [Figures 13, 14]

Figure 13: Sonny Dom Dee, Sal 1962 Bedford Y.M.C.A.

Figure 14: Domenick 1964 Breezy Point

The club made many diving excursions, some from beaches and some from rented boats. The beach dives were family outings. Places such as Shinnecock Inlet, Long Island, and Suntan Lake, New Jersey, provided good skin and scuba diving plus picnic areas for the families. Funds for boat dives were accumulated from the dues members contributed during the year. There were many such dives. One is worth mentioning.

In the summer of 1963, Domenick arranged to take a group of members out for a deep-water dive. They rented a twenty-five foot boat out of Sheepshead Bay, Brooklyn. Onboard were Salvatore, Sonny, John, Dee, Johnny, and Domenick. A few days before this trip it was reported in the newspaper that a man had been attacked by a shark off Sandy Hook, New Jersey. Sandy Hook happened to be about two miles from the area chosen for this club dive. Members voiced their concerns. Domenick stated that two miles is a long way off, and he felt that everything would be fine. Everyone was excited to make this trip as they had never made a deep-water dive. Domenick, being a former Navy Frogman, had plenty of experience.

On their way to the Ambrose Lighthouse Ship the metal shaft of the inboard engine got entangled with a fisherman's monofilament line. The monofilament had wound completely around the three foot metal shaft and stalled the engine. This was one freak accident in a million. Domenick, who was still dressed in his street clothes, asked one of the men in their bathing suits to dive over the side of the boat and investigate the trouble. No one moved. Again Domenick asked someone to inspect the bottom of the boat. Again no one responded. Domenick knew that they were worried about sharks. He got undressed and put on his diving mask and flippers and dove over the side of the boat. Upon inspecting the bottom of the boat he saw the tightly-wound monofilament around the metal shaft. He surfaced and asked for his diving knife. He dove under the boat and after a number of cuts freed the shaft from the line. Domenick boarded the boat and while drying himself with a towel a large fin broke out of the water and circled the boat. It was so close you could have touched the fin with your hand. It was an eight-foot Mako Shark. Domenick froze as he thought he was just in the water a minute ago. Everyone in the boat was so excited that they yelled and jumped around in the boat. Domenick just stood still and stared at the circling fin.

This brought back a vivid memory of the time Domenick served in the Navy during WWII as a Frogman with the U.D.T. While on a three-mile swim parallel to the beach an eight-foot dark gray Bull Shark was trailing him and his Team buddy, James Locksey. When the men stopped to take a routine rest from swimming, the shark began circling them. Seeing that large fin circling was frightening, and the circles got tighter. Suddenly the shark homed in on Domenick and brushed him in passing. It is said that when a shark brushes its prey it will attack on the next pass. Seeing his buddy in trouble, Locksey began frantically splashing the water. This drew the shark's attention away from Domenick. And a miracle happened. The shark swam pass Locksey without attacking and swam away out to sea. Only God knows why, and perhaps he was with them that day. Stunned, the two men cheered and hugged each other. This incident made Jim Locksey and Domenick blood brothers for life.

It was said later that the noise on the metal shaft, which Domenick was cutting loose the monofilament, attracted the shark.

Domenick composed himself and successfully started the engine. He proceeded beyond the Ambrose Lighthouse Ship to deep water. When they were in the deep he had the anchor dropped. He organized the men into pairs to dive with the buddy system. Each pair was to descend a safety line to the bottom, approximately one hundred feet, and then ascend to the surface. Previously taught safety procedures would be followed.

No one moved. Domenick knew that the shark encounter had made the men reluctant to go into the water. He knew that if they didn't make this dive it would be the end of the Aqua Knights Diving Club. He said that he would go down even if he had to do it alone. Domenick knew that his brother Salvatore would never let him do the dive alone. The Cardinal Rule of scuba diving was *always dive with a buddy!* Salvatore and Domenick put on their scuba gear. When Salvatore and Domenick reached the depth of 100 feet it was pitch black. Visibility was only obtained by their hand held diver lights, which they used to read their depth gauges on their wrists. They smiled at each other and gave the OK sign. "Mission Accomplished." They ascended to the surface safely. The other men seeing the successful diving exercise took their turns making the dive. The trip was a great one and everyone had an adventurous story to tell. In the next two years the Aqua Knights Club members made numerous successful dives.

During the three years of the club's existence there were only five unpleasant incidents which could have been tragic. The Mako shark incident, as described, was one. On four other occasions Domenick had to save the life of a member. The first mishap happened under the Mill Basin Bridge in Brooklyn, in twenty feet of water. A diver became stuck in the mud and was dizzy and disoriented. In the murky water, Domenick found him and brought him to the surface safely. In the second incident, a diver got caught in a strong current and was being pulled out to sea. He was completely exhausted when Domenick reached him and together they made the long swim back to the beach. Thirdly, a diver was being battered against the jetty rocks in Shinnecock Inlet, Long island. Domenick grabbed him and pulled him to safety. The fourth incident occurred on a deep wreck dive out of Montauk. A diver panicked and ditched his equipment over the wreck. His discarded weight belt caught on one of his flippers, causing him to sink deeper. Domenick saw something wrong and dove off the chartered boat. He swam down and brought the man to the surface.

More details of these stories is reserved for Domenick to tell in person. Unfortunately, the Aqua Knights Diving Club disbanded in 1965 when Domenick was transferred to work in the Long Beach Naval Shipyard in California.

Another passion of Domenick's, which was becoming too expensive, was to rent riding horses. As a boy he had worked in stables just to be able to ride horses. His most memorable riding events were when he taught and rode with his wife, Vickie. The first time he had taken Vickie to ride had been in Prospect Park, and it had been a comical sight. The horse she was riding was slow but had his own head. While on the bridle path the horse felt it needed a drink. It simply walked off the path and into the nearby lake, up to his knees, lowered his head, and began to drink. Vickie began to panic. She screamed at Domenick to make the horse listen.

"Just let him drink a little, then pull on the reins." Domenick gently coached her to use the reins. She finally did this and the horse walked out from the lake. After much discussion and instructions she gained control of the horse. The rest of the day they had fun.

The next time Vickie rode a horse was on their honeymoon. She had no problem handling the horse. In later years Domenick found a place where you could ride horses on the beach. It was an area in the Canarsie section of Brooklyn called Plum Beach. There were two riding stables from which you could rent horses, Circle G, and Ryan's. Domenick favored Circle G as they had western saddles, plus the owner allowed him to use one of the horses to teach his children to ride. Whenever he took the children horseback riding he would come home dead tired. Even though he was in great shape, walking on the hot sand around large coral, giving instructions to each child on how to ride, was tiring. Although exhausting, Domenick felt real proud when his girls rode horses by themselves. Vickie went horseback riding with him and she enjoyed riding along the beach. It was beautiful to ride together, except for one time.

On a balmy summer day, the horses were feeling frisky. Domenick had told the owner of Circle G that although Vickie knew how to ride, she needed a slow and gentle horse. Vickie and Domenick rode the whole length of Plum Beach. The beach path ended at the Marine Parkway Bridge. When they reached the bridge and turned to return to the stable, Vickie's horse bolted and started to run like the wind. The guess is that the horse sensed it was going home and he was hungry. Domenick tried to catch up to Vickie but it seemed like a stalemate. No matter how hard he pushed his horse he couldn't gain on her. They were traveling at the same speed. A stalemate. Vickie yelled for Domenick for help to stop the horse. The only thing he could yell back was "Hang on!" He prayed she would.

A man with his little son was carrying an outboard

motor across the beach and they were right in the path of the runaway horse. Vickie screamed for them to get out of the way. Domenick saw the fear on their faces as they dropped the motor and ran for their lives. Vickie and horse whizzed right past them. Domenick prayed that she would hang on long enough to reach the asphalt road. It would be at the road that the horse would surely slow down, and he might get control of it. It worked as he had hoped. Her horse slowed up and he was able to grab the bridle and rein it in. From then on the horse was as gentle as a lamb. Vickie rode the horse the rest of the way to the stable. At the stable, Domenick gave her a big hug.

"You rode like a real cowboy."

"Yeah." And she handed him a handful of hair from the horse's mane.

In 1963 an offer was made to Domenick by his in-laws, Frank and Josephine Nigro, to move into their house in Bellrose. They had moved to Florida in 1960 and had rented their house to a doctor. This doctor used the house as an office and examination/clinic. He didn't maintain the house or grounds for three years. The doctor moved out, leaving the home and grounds in a shamble and the property unkempt. The roof leaked, walls had large holes because of testing equipment (X-rays, etc.), the basement had a flood, rooms needed painting, the kitchen was filthy, and floors were worn. The house needed a lot of work. Outside, hedges were overgrown and two large trees in the rear were uprooted. The deal that was offered was if Domenick would fix-up the house and grounds, plus pay the mortgage and expenses, he and Vickie and the children could move in anytime. What was not said is that the in-laws would live in Florida but would visit and stay for the summer.

Domenick struggled with this decision to move, as he knew the consequences of renovating the abused home and property. The time and labor he would have to devote to bring the house back to normal would be tremendous. Also the expense to maintain the house, travel time to the Brooklyn Navy yard, and a host of other unknowns were mindboggling. But for the sake of the children, Domenick agreed to move. It should be mentioned that a few weeks after the offer made by his in-laws to move into their vacant house, an incident occurred which influenced his final decision.

It was the time Toni, his oldest daughter, was almost attacked by an adult Hispanic male. Toni and her neighborhood girlfriend, both ten years old, were playing in the other girl's backyard. This perverted man was watching the little girls through a ten-foot chain link fence, which separated Taffee Place Park from the yard. The man climbed over the fence and approached the two young girls. He tried to talk Spanish to them. His appearance frightened the girls out of their wits and they ran into the hallway of the house. This hallway had two doors, an outer door, a foyer, and an inner door. This animal of a man attempted to push his way through the inner door but he was blocked by Toni, who had wedged her body between the inner door and the post bannister of the staircase. She put her back against the bannister and her feet against the door. Her girlfriend ran screaming upstairs to her mother. The mother in turn came running downstairs yelling, which alerted the rest of the apartment house. With this the man ran back and climbed over the fence and disappeared. It was Toni's quick thinking and strength which held this animal at bay while her friend went for help.

Toni's mother and relatives were in a panic. When Domenick came home from work, only minutes after this incident, he was in a rage. After consoling Toni and her friend, and jotting down the complete story with a description of the man, Domenick and Louie, the other girl's father, went cruising to see if they could spot this man. While cruising the area, Domenick and Louie continued to gently console the little girls, assuring them that they were safe. As difficult as it was, both men kept a calm atmosphere for the sake of the girls. After cruising for a while they concluded that this animal of a man had hidden somewhere. They decided to bring it to the attention of the police and let them handle it.

Domenick and Louie went to the 88th Precinct police Station, which was only two blocks away from their apartments. Both men described the incident and wanted to register a complaint. The desk Sergeant said he can't take the complaint as you have to have a name of the person who committed the crime. Domenick's patience was running out and he explained that whatever the technicalities of the law were, he wanted the police to find this man, as he feels a crime has been committed. The Sergeant replied, "Are you sure that this story is not just a figment of these two girls' imagination?" Domenick lost his cool and began shouting. With that the Sergeant threatened to lock him up. Louie calmed Domenick and said, "You know the cops never help us in this area." Both men left the police station and for a week they and two other friends cruised the area. In one way it was good that they didn't find this man, as God knows what the outcome would have been.

The decision to move came hard, but what made it

easier was the incident in which Toni almost got hurt. That fact and the thought of another incident happening to either of his five daughters being frightened was more than enough to move out of Brooklyn. It is funny as Domenick put it, "We were four generations in the neighborhood and now we're being pushed out. The area was always tough but good and safe, but now it's tough and bad." Domenick's mother and father and most of Domenick's relatives had moved out of the area. Even the Blacks on the block had moved to the Fort Greene projects. Everyone was slowly being scattered about. The glue that held families, people and neighborhoods together was coming apart. That's progress for you!

It is to be noted that the original offer to move into the Bellrose house appeared to be a good gesture, but in reality was exploitation. So the summer of 1963 in which the Scarlato family moved from Brooklyn to Queens was an adventure in itself.

Domenick's brother-in-law, Dennis, volunteered to help him move and that he would get his boss' truck. Vickie had reservations about the move and asked Dennis is he positive he can get the truck. Dennis assured her he would take care of everything. It was a great idea, and all being young and strong the move would be a snap. Also it could help save moving expenses as the Scarlato's certainly could use the money, especially since Domenick had spent over a month renovating the neglected house and property in Bellrose. He went every night and weekend to work on the house and the grounds.

Even though the Scarlato's didn't have a great deal of household items, it was still a hard job packing and preparing for the move by a scheduled date. When everything was in order and the scheduled date was near, Domenick asked Dennis to have the truck ready for that weekend. At the last minute Dennis told Domenick that he could not get the truck, and that he could not help as he had another commitment. This left Vickie and Domenick in a very nervous bind, as they were scheduled to vacate their apartment by a set date. Domenick frantically tried to get a moving company, which was not the best, to agree to move them on the scheduled date but they must be paid by the hour. Domenick had no choice and agreed.

On the scheduled date the moving company did not show up at the appointed time of 9:00 A.M. in the morning. They arrived at 8:00 P.M. at night. Domenick was furious. He had no choice but to allow the move to commence. Obviously these moving men had worked all day moving another family, or families, and they were tired. When they would move an item it was in slow motion with a lot of breaks. The moving company was being paid by the hour; consequently, the owner did not care how long they took. This made Domenick very nervous, but he had to remain calm as he did not want to upset his wife and children. In fact, he tried to speed up the move as he himself carried many items three flights downstairs to the truck. It was 12:00 A.M. in the morning when the truck was finally loaded and it took off for Bellrose. Vickie and Domenick felt like gypsies stealing away in the night as they drove to Bellrose. The move was finally completed and the truck was empty by 3:00 A.M. in the morning. The children and Vickie were exhausted, and they were sleeping in their station wagon. When the owner of the moving company wanted to be paid off, Domenick deducted two hours from the total amount. The owner started to argue, and Domenick said it was bad enough he moved them in the middle of the night but he tried to drag the job out for all he could. It was a most ridiculous scene with the two men arguing. Domenick offered to settle this disagreement with fists. The mover got into his truck and quickly drove off. This was a lesson well learned by Domenick. In the future he would listen to his wife and be reluctant to trust the word of anyone. He would and did make sure that any future moves were correct and smooth, and they would never be taken advantage of again. He was never taken advantage of again, but a smooth move — well, that's another story.

The bad experience of the move from Brooklyn to Bellrose, because of not getting the truck as promised, did not cause Domenick to hold a grudge. This was a positive trait he inherited from his father.

The year was 1965 and President L. B. Johnson and his "wonder boy" secretary of Defense McNamara decided to close the time honored Brooklyn Navy Yard. This executive order came down on the fifteen thousand Navy Yard workers like "Thor's Hammer." This bolt of lightning shocked not only the yard workers but the Navy Department and including the entire community. This 164 year old Navy Yard was the second largest and most updated and efficient Navy Yard in the world.

To close the Yard was insane, but then again there was a hidden agenda behind President Johnson's motives. Part of the President's agenda was, with the advice of his Wonder Boy, to embrace the private industrial war complex. To favor private industry, to break the unions, to reduce costs for the Department of Defense and revitalize the economy of the South. The President ordered seventy-one bases throughout the northeast part of the United States to close with more than half relocated to the southern part of the United States. Federal workers who qualified were offered and were transferred to other bases and many, too many, were laid off. Federal employees who were laid off had many years of service, and unfortunately they were not covered by unemployment benefits. In 1965 a federal employee was not covered by the Employment Act. They were in effect second class citizens. The base closures caused tremendous hardships on thousands of federal workers as many were uprooted to move south or west or worse lose their jobs. There were men and woman who had more than twenty years of government service, and it was a shame they were not qualified for unemployment benefits nor able to retire. Some had nervous breakdowns and, yes, there were others who literally tried suicide. These were tough times for the shipyard workers.

To understand President Johnson's agenda is very difficult as it was a complex plan evolving with much political history. To try to simplify certain aspects of his plan was to look back before he was Vice President. LBJ was a southern politician who always embraced private enterprises to enhance his career. Also he had always hoped that the South would grow economically. His distaste for easterners, such as the Kennedys, is a matter of record. It is amazing how John Kennedy chose L. B. Johnson as his running mate. It is very strange how politics chooses strange bedfellows. He probably needed the southern vote.

Before President Kennedy was assassinated he had prepared an order to remove five thousand military advisers from Viet Nam. President Kennedy was trying to extricate us from the entanglement of the Viet Nam War. After President Kennedy was assassinated, Vice President Johnson became President. With the help of his very business-like "wonder boy," Secretary of Defense McNamara, he developed his agenda. He embraced the private industrial war complex. President Johnson rescinded President Kennedy's order to remove five thousand advisors. He then increased, by increments, the troops in Viet Nam to over 250,000 plus. There have been reams of papers written about the Viet Nam War as it was fought by the Washington, D.C. bureaucrats. It was President Johnson's war but it was run exclusively by Secretary McNamara and his bureaucrats. This political-industrial war lasted for over ten years and cost over 58,000 dead Americans plus untold number of wounded. The scars of this war will always be with us. In the year 2001 McNamara, to purify his soul, admitted all his mistakes he made towards his country, and especially the Viet Nam War. It is too bad that President Johnson hid his misuse of the Defense Department's operation by cloaking it among other activities. Under his umbrella he called his "Great Society," he pushed for social change. The Civil Rights movement, welfare, entitlements, educational and training—Job Corps, etc. This subject will be addressed in a later chapter, especially the Job Corps.

To relate back to base closures, one may conclude the President jeopardized the national security of America by closing bases. This was not true as other bases in the south and west were expanded plus the private sector received much more work. For instance in the case of the Brooklyn Navy Yard, it was the only naval Shipyard capable of building and servicing supercarriers. The only other shipyard capable of building and servicing supercarriers was Newport News of Virginia, a private shipyard. There was a long-standing congressional law that if a capital ship was built in a private shipyard, then one must be built in a Naval Shipyard. The reason was in the event of a war and a private shipyard had labor problems our country would not be in jeopardy. President Johnson circumvented the law by simply closing the Naval Shipyard, and now the only shipyard capable of building and servicing supercarriers was the Newport News Shipyard of Virginia. Many federal workers tried to fight the decision to close or relocate bases. There were many organized trips to Washington to try to pressure congressmen to have President Johnson rescind this infamous order. Domenick being very involved with the National Association of Government Employees Union helped organize bus trips to Washington. He, along with many other top union officials of other unions, met with a number of Congressmen. All of these Congressmen promised to help, but it was futile. In fact, the carpetbagger Robert Kennedy from Massachusetts was campaigning for U. S. Senator of New York. He held a rally outside the Brooklyn Navy Yard. He promised if he were elected U. S. Senator he would go to President Johnson's office the next day and demand that the Brooklyn Navy yard remain open and operational. How strange it is that a man from Massachusetts can run for a political office in New York. At that time little did the people of New York know that President Johnson hated the Kennedys. Well, Robert Kennedy was elected U. S. Senator from New York, and when he went to President Johnson's office it is said that he was thrown out, figuratively speaking. Needless to say the Brooklyn Navy Yard was scheduled to close along with many others. Although the national security wasn't jeopardized, the crime was that it cost the taxpayers hundreds of millions of dollars and devastated the employment rate in the Northeast for a number of years.

President Johnson's policy of closing and

relocating military bases throughout the Northeastern part of the United States would cause over 173,000 people to be unemployed. Of that amount there would be 15,000 Navy Yard people unemployed locally. This was a heavy burden to bear on the many people who served the Department of Defense so loyally. Congress tried to ease this economic burden by passing a law that would have the operating bases to offer jobs to qualified candidates who were willing to relocate. The government would pay the cost of moving the candidate's family. There were three Welder Combination Mechanic positions offered at the Long Beach Naval Shipyard in California. Since there were no jobs for Instructors throughout the country, Domenick seriously thought about applying for this position. It was a reduction and you must relocate, but to be unemployed with five children was something Domenick could not bear. He spoke at length with Vickie and his children. It was a big move and this made Domenick and Vickie very nervous, but to continue his career in government service was important. The children were excited, especially to see Disney World.

Domenick spoke with the Master of his Shop, Mr. Stuchell, and he advised Domenick to apply for this position. Mr. Stuchell was the Master of Shop 26, with a staff of more than 1,300 personnel, yet he knew Domenick's impeccable record. He not only advised Domenick to apply for this position, but he gave him a strong letter of recommendation. Mr. Stuchell also advised Domenick that after he settles in at Long Beach Naval Shipyard to ask for an appointment to see the Master of the Shop. He said to be bold but gracious and show the Master the letter of recommendation. Mr. Stuchell said with Domenick's record, ambition, and future performance, he would move up the ladder in Long Beach. It is said that Mr. Stuchell never gives letters of recommendation, but Domenick was well liked and respected by Mr. Stuchell.

After much soul-searching, Domenick again spoke with his wife, and also with his mother- and father-in-law. The decision was made and Domenick applied for the Welding Combination mechanic's position. Domenick was quickly accepted for this position, and now the journey to California was the start of an adventure never to be forgotten by the Scarlato family. Now the preparation to travel and move began. Domenick began to sell various items not needed in California, such as snow tires, chains, certain furniture, etc. he made plans on driving cross-country and where to live while working in California. He researched numerous items and planned every detail possible. Since he was going to live in California he would constantly research areas where the family could settle and be happy. When Domenick felt the work was completed in California, he will send for Vickie, Toni, Linda and Diana, and they too will give their insights as to how and where to live. They would fly American Airlines at government expense. Barbara and Darlene, because of their young age, will stay in Bellrose with their grandparents, Josephine and Frank Nigro. When the major move was to take place, Vickie would fly back to New York and then come back to California with Barbara and Darlene.

SEVEN
California

Domenick teamed up with a Shipfitter named John Foley. John was also selected to work at the Long beach Naval Shipyard and was to share the driving and expenses of the trip to California. Domenick planned the trip to take five days and tried to cover approximately seven hundred miles a day. The plan was to stop at a scenic place and stay in a reasonable motel. Domenick allowed himself two weeks to travel to California. This would allow him enough time in the event there was a delay such as a storm, a breakdown or whatever. Also this would give him the time to rent a room at the YMCA and explore the area before reporting to work. John Foley only allowed himself one week for the trip. Domenick didn't like his decision but compromised and both embarked on May 20, 1965, for California. Although Domenick had a 1959 Chevrolet Station Wagon, he did not overload it. He traveled light but he took one hunting rifle and a shotgun for a possible hunt and for protection.

The first third of the trip was pleasant as they traveled mostly Thruways and Turnpike, but the rest of the trip they traveled on Route 66. Route 66 was a two lane highway with plenty of trucks. Traveling was both slow and fast depending on conditions. They did hit some bad rain squalls, but managed to survive the heavy rains and floods. An incident which disturbed Domenick was in Texas. There was a terrible tornado which decimated a small town. Over the radio they heard a plea for anyone with a truck or station wagon to please come help the many people who were seriously hurt. They badly needed help to transport these afflicted people to hospitals. Since Domenick and John were not far from this town, Domenick wanted to volunteer his services and his station wagon, but John talked him out of it. He said there was no time to spare as he had only a week to report to work. He said to stop would jeopardize his job. Domenick said "Too bad you only planned for a week."

This incident among other conversations made Domenick realize that John was a friend he could do without. They arrived in Long beach as planned, and Domenick rented a room at the YMCA, as it was very clean, reasonably priced, and he could use the gym facilities. John said he wanted a room in which he could bring guests to visit him. Domenick helped him find such a room and that was the last time Domenick ever saw John.

Domenick spent the next week adjusting to his surroundings and cruised the area for familiarization. He reported to the Long Beach Naval Shipyard on time, and he began the difficult adjustment to work among men who felt that the "easterners" were put ahead of them on the retention list due to seniority. This was not Domenick's imagination. He could tell by some of the slips of their words in his many conversations with the Yard workers. Also the work assignments he received from his supervisor were not fair. One example is Domenick was assigned to weld the scuppers on the side of the ship. Domenick stood on a platform which was lowered by the Riggers by pulleys on to the side of the ship. While welding these scuppers, at times waste-water with turds would overspill the scuppers onto Domenick. He was furious. He called to have the platform raised so he could complain that the toilet must be secured. He called and yelled many times and no one responded. After about two hours his supervisor admonished Domenick for not completing the assigned job. Domenick in a calm voice asked to have the platform raised. As he stepped off he calmly laced into the supervisor about him being doused by the waste-water and turds from the toilets. Why didn't he have the toilets secured? The supervisor was white-faced and he apologized to Domenick. There were other incidents such as working in the bilges or high on a mast and so on. Through it all, Domenick managed to get along with most of the workers. In fact, he was invited by some old time yard workers to have dinner at their houses. He slowly gained their acceptance and respect because of his competence and as a person.

Every night after work Domenick would map out an area to research. After work he would travel to each area or town to check out their homes, schools, hospitals, etc. He would record all this information in a looseleaf, and also gather any materials concerning the town in question. He visited each town from Hollywood south almost to San Diego. Domenick's favorite town was La Jolla, but it was a little too far and very expensive. There were many good towns but overall, at that time, Huntington Beach appeared to be a good choice, but time would tell. The rest of the family must agree. Domenick also took in the sights which he knew Vickie and the children would enjoy. He visited various beaches, the desert, Disney World, and many local sights, including all the way down to Tijuana, Mexico.

After six weeks of working, researching, and numerous letters to Vickie, Domenick looked for a temporary furnished apartment for Vickie and his three children. He found a beautiful four-room furnished apartment with a pool in a small garden Apartment Complex. This complex was on Locust Avenue and one block off Long Beach Blvd. Now it was time for Vickie, Toni, Linda and Diana, to come to California. [Figure 15]

Figure 15: Linda, Toni, Diana 1965

The plane touched down at the Los Angeles Airport, July 10, 1965, and out stepped the rays of sunshine Domenick was anxiously waiting for. Vickie, Toni, Linda and Diana, simultaneously hugged Domenick. The hug was so hard that tears flowed like Niagara Falls from each and every individual. After much kissing and hugging, the Scarlato family drove to their new furnished apartment. During the drive, Vickie and the girls updated Domenick on all the things he had missed back home and how wonderful their airplane trip was. Upon arriving at the apartment, Vickie and the children were very surprised at its beauty and overwhelmingly gave their approval. The girls quickly went for a swim in the pool before dinner. Domenick drove the family for a sightseeing tour of Long beach. He showed them where to go shopping, the Navy Yard, the beaches, etc. With Vickie familiar with the area she could drive Domenick to work in the morning and pick him up in the evening. In this way Vickie had use of the station wagon during the day to shop, go to the beach, or just explore.

One day Domenick asked his supervisor for permission to see the Master of the Shop. The supervisor nervously asked, "For what purpose?" Domenick replied, "It is personal." The supervisor gave him a pass to go to the main office. When Domenick arrived at the main office he asked the secretary to see Mr. Franchel. She said he was busy, but when Domenick showed her the letter from Mr. Stuchell, she immediately went into his office. Within five minutes Domenick was allowed into the master's office. Upon seeing Mr. Franchel, Domenick became very nervous. This man was at least 6'4" tall and very gruff. He and Domenick talked at length. The Master was very impressed not only with the letter by Mr. Stuchell, but especially their lengthy talk. He said that he would give Domenick a personal tour of the Navy Yard and that they could talk some more. They walked through the various buildings where parts of ships were being constructed. Also they walked around the docks where the ships were tied up. Many Yard workers took note of this. The Master told Domenick he could have a bright future in the Navy Yard. He said he had five instructors in the Apprentice School and one is an alcoholic close to the age of retirement. He told Domenick that with his background and organizational skills he could be an asset to the Yard, and he could easily qualify for an Instructor position. Also with the blessings of Mr. Franchel, Domenick could not miss being appointed as an Instructor of Apprentices. Domenick graciously thanked the Master for the tour of the Navy Yard and the time he spent with him. He returned to the ship he was working on and reported back to the supervisor. The supervisor asked Domenick why it took over two hours to talk to the master. Domenick was never one to brag or drop names. He just smiled and said that they had a lot to talk about. It goes without saying that within a couple of days, Domenick's work assignments were given to him in a fairer manner.

Vickie and the children used to drive Domenick back and forth to work in heavy traffic. Before reaching the Long Beach Naval Shipyard they had to cross over a pontoon bridge, which was hilly. At first this bridge disturbed Vickie, but in time she got used to this floating, hilly bridge. When Vickie drove the station wagon without Domenick the car sometimes stalled, and it took a long time to start again. Domenick told her if the car stalled just open the hood and tap the side of the carburetor with a small hammer and the wagon would start again. Domenick said when he can have a day off he will have the carburetor fixed. One day Vickie was driving on Long beach Boulevard and the car stalled at a red light. The light turned green and the other cars started to beep their horns. Vickie became very nervous and before she knew it there were two men pushing the wagon to the side of the road. They offered to help Vickie—who had her three girls in the car. Vickie replied, "No, I have the situation well in hand." The two men watched her open the hood and tap the carburetor with the small hammer. She then proceeded to start the car and thanked the men for their help. Both men scratched their heads and said, "Boy! What a mechanic." Vickie just smiled and drove off. Another comical scene used to occur at the Navy yard. After Vickie dropped off Domenick inside the Navy Yard perimeter, she would have to drive out through the Main Gate. Even though there was a traffic light outside the gate, there was a motorcycle cop posted there to direct the heavy traffic. When he saw Vickie coming he knew she was going to stall. So, he would immediately stop all traffic and wave his hand frantically allowing Vickie to pass the red light. Domenick eventually had the station wagon fixed, and for the remainder of their stay they never had another problem.

Every day Vickie took the children somewhere. Either sightseeing or the beach. When they came home from the beach they went into the pool. The girls liked to swim in the pool before lunch. After supper Domenick would take the family for sightseeing of different towns and areas of southern California. He wanted them to have firsthand knowledge of each area so when it came time to choose where to settle permanently it would be to everyone's liking. On weekends Domenick and the family took pleasure trips to Disney World, Sea World, museums, Hollywood, and even Tijuana, Mexico. In Tijuana the family went to see a Bull Fight. Their seats were high up in the stands and the stands were nothing more than pipes bolted together. When the people yelled at the Matador the stands would shake. Besides being uneasy sitting in these seats, witnessing a bull fight was disgusting and brutal. The bull never had a chance. He was doomed to die before he ever entered the ring. There were supposed to be twelve bull fights. The Scarlatos left after the first. Shopping in Tijuana was fruitful. They bought costume jewelry, a leather pocketbook, and two 3'tall Siamese cat statues that the children wanted. That evening when the Scarlatos were going through the Customs gate on the U.S. side of the border, an Immigration officer questioned who the twins belong to. The twins had waist-length dark hair in braids and beautiful tans from the beach. Domenick said they were his children. The officer asked the girls who their parents were and where were they born. They both simultaneously answered that these are our parents and we were born in Brooklyn, New York. After hearing them speak, the Immigration officer smiled and said, "Go ahead, and good luck."

The trip to Tijuana was pleasant as Vickie and the children saw La Hoya, San Diego, plus the countryside. Of the thousands of questions the children asked Domenick there was one that always stuck in his head. What were those giant grasshoppers all over southern California? Domenick explained they weren't giant grasshoppers but oil pumps which go up and down pumping oil from oil wells. There were no oil derricks in southern California, but oil pumps that looked and moved their heads like giant grasshoppers.

During their stay in California, Domenick made many friends, but a few were worth associating with. There was a young Shipfitter named John Elliot who was married to a Samoan girl and they had five children. Before Vickie and the girls came, Elliot (he liked to be called by his last name) and Domenick used to frequent a few bars. One such place was called the Fort Apache. This bar was built in the image of an 1870 fort and inside had Go-Go dancing girls. Some suspended in cages and some on a small stage. They wore short-shorts, boots, and halters. This seemed to be the uniform of the 1960's. The Go-Go dancing craze started in California and any bar you went to had a Go-Go dancer. Another bar that Elliot took Domenick to was in the town of Compton. To say that the town of Compton was put on a map was because of a case that was brought before the Supreme Court. When Domenick entered this bar he had a strange feeling that this was not an ordinary bar. There were two huge men at the door, which were probably bouncers. As Domenick and Elliot sat down, Domenick noticed that there were no women in the place. Domenick said to himself, is this a place for queers? If so, why the bouncers? A woman's voice said to Domenick, "What will you have?" Domenick turned to see where this voice came from and lo and behold, there stood a young beautiful waitress with her breasts exposed bare. Domenick almost fell off the chair. Now he knew why the bouncers were there. Elliot laughed so hard he did fall off his chair. Elliot deliberately took Domenick to Compton to shake him up, and shake him up it did. The owner of that bar in Compton was later arrested. He took his case all the way to the U.S. Supreme Court and won. That in 1965 started the trend for topless bars throughout the U. S. A.

Domenick used to frequent a certain diner to eat supper. In this diner was a beautiful waitress who treated Domenick like family. On their first encounter Domenick had ordered a double order of toast and coffee. The waitress said to Domenick, "You said coffee." Domenick asked, "What's wrong?" She said excitedly, "You're from New York. I know that because we New Yorkers speak like that." Yes, both were from Brooklyn and that started a good friendship. In fact, she used to charge him half price for his meals. She introduced Domenick to her husband. Her name was Trudy, and his Frank Connolly. When Vickie and the children were in California, the Connollys invited them to dinner. They had a beautiful house in Long Beach. Frank, who was good looking, worked as a bartender in the Disney World Hotel. He asked Domenick how much he made at the Navy Yard. When Domenick told Frank, he laughed and said that he could double that salary just with the tips at the bar. Frank said that a lot of women frequented the bar and they tip big. Many tips double the bill and more. Frank said to Domenick that with his looks and personality he could really make it big as a bartender at Disney World. He told Domenick if he ever needs a job or changes his mind, he could help him get a job as a bartender. He would even teach him. It was obvious that Frank really liked Domenick, and at that time New Yorkers did stick together. An example how their home state meant something.

One day Domenick was driving on Long Beach Blvd, and when he stopped at a light, he saw a man in the rear-view mirror running towards him and yelling, "Wait up! Wait up!" When this man approached Domenick's open window, he said breathlessly, "You are from New York, I see your license plate and you are from New York." He added in a happy voice, "I'm from New York too." Domenick pulled the station wagon to the side of the road and began talking to the man. The man's name was Joe Fiorenzo and he said he was in real estate. He told Domenick if he ever needed a job to contact him and he will get him into real estate.

Domenick really liked California and these positive encounters reinforced this belief. Unfortunately there was a negative side. There was smog, especially from Los Angeles, and the tremors from the San Andreas Fault. But they were thirty-five miles from Los Angeles and the smog wasn't too bad. The tremors — well, they pretend it is the subway under them. These things seemed tolerable since there were many other positive things.

A very shocking announcement blared over the radio. It was that a riot was in progress in the Watts area of Los Angeles. This was a predominately Black area. Domenick turned on the television and there was a clear view of stores being looted, cars being overturned and complete turmoil on the streets. The police tried their best to contain the riot in a small area, but it spread rapidly. By nightfall the television showed buildings on fire. There was an aerial view of the city and it showed a pattern to these fires. One set of fires in the North section, another in the South section, and both east and West had fires. It looked as though this was not a random riot, but a riot planned by some group. Who planned this devastation, which looked more like an insurrection than a riot, was anyone's guess. The National Guard was called in to suppress this supposed riot. The General of the National Guard made an announcement on television and over the radio, that this was an insurrection and he needed the Army to help him. The destruction carried into the next day. In Long Beach, as well as many other areas, there were small pockets of destruction taking place.

Long Beach Boulevard had over a hundred new and used car dealerships strung out along the highway. By the afternoon not one car could be seen on the lots. The boulevard was completely deserted. It was said that all of the cars had been shipped to the desert for protection. When Domenick and Vickie went shopping they saw people carrying sidearms. Women wheeling baby carriages were wearing sidearms. Seeing this Domenick loaded his shotgun and carried it in the station wagon. At home he kept it close by. Vickie was also well versed in how to use firearms. It was to be noted that the media reported that anyone who was armed did not have their stores or homes attacked or destroyed. Armed citizens were able to protect their property. This insurrection announcement by the National Guard General was later changed. It was then called a riot by the Mayor of Los Angeles and the Governor of California. This was hard for Domenick to believe as he had witnessed firsthand the pattern of the destruction. The large amount of destruction in various areas could never happen at random. It had to have been coordinated by some group. It was definitely planned, but why did the General change his statement? A small article on the back page of a newspaper said that if the destruction was caused by an insurrection then the insurance companies were not obligated to pay for the damages. If the destruction was caused by a riot, then they had to pay. The business community and the politicians forced the General to change his statement. This seems to be a plausible explanation, but it is unfortunate because the planners of this destruction got away with looting, burning and injuring numerous people.

This infamous incident became known as the Watts Riot, and many businesses and politicians bowed to the numerous demands of the Black leaders. Domenick, Vickie, and the children drove through many streets and areas and saw the devastation. These experiences left a nightmarish impression on them. This infamous incident put a permanent stain on southern California's history.

The Watts Riot put an uneasy feeling of living in California, but as time passed things slowly returned to normal. Domenick went to work, the girls enjoyed the pool, Vickie and the children relaxed on the beach. All was well until...One day Vickie asked Domenick if he would drive himself to work, as she wasn't feeling too well and wanted to stay home. The children could amuse themselves in the pool. Domenick agreed and said he would pick up some food at Jack-in-the-Box so Vickie could relax. That evening when Domenick came home from work he found Vickie as white as a sheet, and the children were very quiet.

"What's wrong," he asked her. "Are you all right?"

"Go and look at the pool."

Domenick went and checked the pool. To his horror he saw a huge pole partially in the pool, and the pool was completely black. There was a smell of burnt rubber in the air. He realized that the pole was an electrical pole which provided power to the homes. He went back to Vickie.

"What happened?"

She explained. "Thank God our children are well behaved and came immediately when I called. The girls were in the pool having fun. It was close to lunchtime and I called out to them to come inside to eat. They did not dilly-dally. They quickly got out of the pool and were walking inside when the whole complex started to shake..."

They were experiencing an earthquake. The electrical pole broke loose and came crashing down into the pool, which created a tremendous noise with sparks flying. To think if the children had stayed another minute in the pool they would have been electrocuted. Three beautiful girls would have been lost.

Vickie said to Domenick that this could be an omen which should be heeded. "We were never meant to be here. We must go back to New York!" She was on the brink of hysteria.

Domenick calmed her down and assured her that they would leave California and go back home.

The next day Domenick went directly to the Personnel Office and submitted his resignation.

The Master of the Shop heard that Domenick was resigning and asked him to come to his office. The Master asked if he was resigning because of harassment. Domenick said, no, and proceeded to tell him the story of the pool, which had almost killed his three girls. He said that after the riots and the earthquake his wife could not bear to live here. Domenick said his family's health and wellbeing came before anything else.

The Master was very understanding and assured Domenick that if he ever changed his mind he would rehire him. Domenick thanked him for all the courtesy which he had extended. Domenick went home and told Vickie to call her mother.

"You can tell her that we are preparing to come home."

Now, to prepare for the long journey home.

The trip to New York would be long, and could be tedious and boring. Domenick had to plan the trip to be interesting and as pleasant as he could make it. He planned to travel no more than 600 miles a day. They would stop at Holiday Inns throughout the trip. Holiday Inns were clean and had pools. They would try to rest near scenic areas. If possible, they would spend an entire day at the more important scenic sites, such as the Grand Canyon, the Petrified Forest, Painted Desert, etc. Domenick went to Sears and purchased a roof rack, at tarp, rope, a cooler, water jug, and a water bag. The water bag was to hang in front of the car when crossing the desert. He also purchased a large, soft mat to lay in the back of the wagon with two pillows and a blanket. He took the children to purchase reading books, art books, coloring books, and games to play,

The station wagon already had necessary emergency equipment such as a jack, tools, flashlights, and minor spare parts. Since the wagon had no air conditioner, Domenick had bypassed the heater and used the fan only to cool the car when crossing the desert. He loaded almost everything onto the roof rack, the main luggage, scuba tanks and gear, the two large Siamese cat sculptures, souvenirs, etc. Specially planned changes of clothing, toiletries, and personal items were put into small bags and placed on the rack where they could be easily obtained. Plenty of room remained in the 1959 Impala Station Wagon. Cooler, water jug, and entertainment items were easily accessible in the wagon.

The Scarlato family finally embarked on their adventurous journey across the United States. The plan worked perfect. They stayed at Holiday Inns and swam in their pools. They saw many interesting sights. To drive through towns and cities is interesting, but to travel through the Mohave Desert is awesome. When they stopped to cool the engine, Domenick would guide the children very closely. This was to avoid any rattlesnake that may be under a rock. The children explored the area and saw various kinds of cacti which were blooming beautiful small flowers. They saw lizards, prairie dogs and other small animals. The only part of traveling through the desert which was not too pleasant was a rainstorm that was so heavy that Domenick had to stop the car and wait it out. Lightning struck all around them and looked and sounded like artillery fire. The wagon shook. One of the girls remarked that the storm is beautiful in a horrible way.

After driving through the desert they stopped at Needles for gas. This was a small town on the edge of the desert. The young fellow pumping the gas said, "You people are lucky. There's a sandstorm predicted to cross the desert late this afternoon. Sand storms can strip the paint off your car and frost your windows."

Vickie said, "God is with us." And they proceeded

on their way.

The countryside continually changed. When they went through the mountain pass everything was a vivid green. As they came down into Arizona they were again in a desert. Traveling through Arizona desert was interesting but it appeared more barren. When they traveled up into the Arizona mountains the terrain turned emerald green with big evergreen trees and lush green fields. Near the town of Flagstaff they saw herds of Pronghorn Antelope.

At the Grand Canyon, Vickie and the children were speechless. It was the most breathtaking sight anyone could ever see. They spent the whole day at the Canyon. Domenick, in his prankish way, played a not too nice joke on Vickie and his girls. He spied a small edge below the upper edge of the Canyon cliff. No one else noticed it. Domenick said, "I've had it. I'm ending it all." And with that he jumped off the cliff. Vickie and the girls screamed. And with that he poked his head up and climbed back onto the Canyon cliff/ Everyone started punching Domenick, who was laughing so hard that he fell to the ground. They all started to laugh, but they made Domenick promise to never pull a stunt like that again. He apologized and promised.

They proceeded on to the Petrified Forest. This is a National Park which protects the most unique trees in the world. It took millions of years to fossilize the trees and turn them into stone. They appear exactly as they did millions of years ago. The only way to tell they are not trees is by touching them. Vickie was so moved by this geological phenomenon that she took a ten inch x six inch piece of petrified wood and wrapped it into her sweater. After they had driven a few miles, she showed Domenick her souvenir. Domenick was shocked and he jammed on the brakes.

"Didn't you read the sign that said, 'Anyone taking any piece of petrified wood will be fined $5,000 and get one year in jail? It's a federal Offense!"

Vickie's only words were that she was so fascinated by the petrified wood, and there were so many huge pieces laying around, that she had to have a small piece. "Who will miss a small piece?"

"That is no small piece. It must weigh five pounds." Domenick added, "You are our Saint who never would dare take anything that didn't belong to you...But then again, anyone can be tempted."

"I promise I'll never be tempted again."

Domenick couldn't bring back the piece of petrified wood, so they kept it. It has been in the family for more than 53 years and it is a cherished memento.

The trip through each state was pleasant and interesting. Vickie and Domenick also tried to make the trip educational. They took time to explain the sights they saw. They also answered any questions the children presented. Although the trip was good, there were some mishaps. The Firestone mishaps were that they suffered three tire blow-outs. One in each state. Domenick had purchased four new Firestone tires before they embarked. He believed them to be the best. Now he had to buy three more tires. You could be sure they were not Firestones. Domenick said he would never buy another Firestone tire and he never did.

Even though their journey had some mishaps and some weather problems, the sights enjoyed by all were unforgettable. They shared pleasures provided a closeness that made a loving bond forever.

The rest of the trip provided fascinating and emotional experiences. Going through numerous tunnels that penetrated the Pennsylvania mountains. Seeing and going over the Verrazano Bridge to Brooklyn. Brooklyn — the place they were born. The closer they got to Queens the greater their anxiety became. No words could describe the emotions when the station wagon drove into the driveway in Bellrose. Barbara came running out with Darlene trailing behind her. They hugged and kissed everyone and began dancing and jumping all around. The excitement was electrifying. Vickie's mother and father hugged and kissed everyone and then cried. Everyone had tears. They were tears of joy. Everyone was so happy to be together again. Domenick said we will never be separated again. [Figure 16, Figure 17]

Figure 16: Barbara 1965

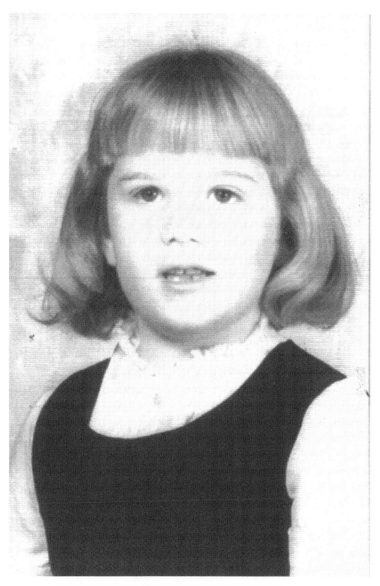

Figure 17: Darlene 1965

The family settled down back to normal life in Bellrose. Vickie began preparing the children for attending school in September. For Domenick all was not normal. The reality was that he was thirty-eight years old and unemployed in a high unemployment area. How will he support his wife and five children? He immediately went to the New York State Employment Office to register and seek employment. The office was located in Jamaica, Queens. At the employment office they told Domenick that teachers and Instructors should report to East 19th Street in Manhattan. This was a long way to travel. He had to take a bus and then the subway for approximately an hour and a half trip. He reported to the Manhattan office and registered. When he was finally interviewed he was told that he was disqualified from employment benefits because he had quit his job. He would have to wait seven weeks before applying for benefits. Domenick was shocked, disappointed, and then angry, but what could he do? He returned home and began searching for a job, any job, in the Want Ads of the newspapers. He became very discouraged. Even though they tightened their belts, their savings was quickly depleted. Vickie said to Domenick not to give up hope and that God will provide.

With that the next day Domenick received a telephone call from Nancy. Nancy was a secretary Domenick knew from the Navy Yard Apprentice School. The school was now closed, and she worked in the Industrial Relations Office. The IRO, as it was called, was a giant Personnel Office with approximately eighty or more people working there. This office handled all the personnel and health records of 15,000 employees. The office processed lay-offs, transfers and relocations of Navy Yard workers. Nancy said to Domenick that she heard through the grapevine that he was back in New York and unemployed. She said that he could be hired as a temporary clerk and work in the IRO office. She said that he could easily get the job because of his past good reputation in the Navy Yard. She said she never forgot him and she knew she had to help him. Domenick was so appreciative for the information, and told her he could not wait to see her in person and thank her. He went to the IRO and he was surprised to see some of the same people he knew from the field. One such person was Joe Bionjovani, who welcomed Domenick with open arms. He processed Domenick's application personally, and said they were only hiring temporary help for a maximum of one year. That's how long it was going to take to process all the 15,000 workers and close the Yard. Domenick told Joe he is grateful for any position.

Joe said he is hired as a GS-5 Clerk and assigned to the Retention Department of the Personnel Office. The Retention Department stored all the records of personnel, listed by seniority. The records had to be processed with extreme accuracy on the job offers, transfers, the R.I.F. (Reduction in Force), etc. all by seniority. It was a complicated procedure but Joe told Domenick he is smart and would catch on quickly. Domenick was very grateful for a chance to at least work. He thanked Joe and went to see Nancy. He thanked her with plenty of hugs. They talked over old times, and then Domenick went home to tell Vickie the good news. It is to be noted that Vickie and Domenick never let their daughters know how serious the situation was, but then they never talked finances or troubles that they may have in front of the children.

Domenick reported bright and early to the Supervisor of the Retention Department. The supervisor's name was John Benson. He found Benson to be very friendly and helpful. Benson slowly took the time to explain the various complicated procedures necessary to handle the great number of workers to be processed. He also teamed Domenick up with a congenial fellow to work together. Domenick wanted to and did learn very fast. In fact he learned more than his job required. He even learned the supervisor's job. In due time it got around that Domenick's competence exceeded many people's expectations. There were fifteen people working in the Retention Section and Domenick got along with all of them famously.

Nat Doctors, who was the IRO Superintendent, was aware of Domenick's initiative, competency, and human relationships. This was because Supervisor John Benson made many positive remarks about Domenick's accomplishments in such a short time to Joe Bionjovani, who in turn mentioned this to the Superintendent. Domenick always took on more responsibility even when not asked. When John Benson was offered a job in Washington, he accepted. This left the position of supervisor open. Domenick was offered that position. Even though Domenick could not be promoted to a GS-9 supervisory level because he was a temporary employee, he accepted the position of Supervisor of the Retention Department. This very responsible position gave him no more money, but he welcomed the challenge.

Domenick knew the staff well and he knew the problems which the department was experiencing. Some examples: An elderly woman who was in charge of the Reproduction Department always called Benson to borrow one or two of the Retention clerks, and he used to accommodate her. This put a burden on Retention department. He also knew that his staff was not happy with this situation. When the woman called Domenick to have two of his clerks come to Reproduction Department, Domenick politely told her he could not afford to have anyone put on loan as his department was very busy. Domenick was fortunate in that even though this woman complained to administration, upper management backed Domenick's decision on how to run his department. This gave Domenick more confidence, and it helped build morale among his staff. Another example of positive change was if an employee refused a job offer, this was recorded on the Retention list and then that employee was vulnerable to be laid off. The problem arose when the employee was off from the job claiming to be sick. They would send a certified letter of the job offer. There were times when the employee did not answer the letter, consequently they were given notice that they were R.I.F. The employee would put in a formal grievance claiming that they were never notified of a job offer. Even though a certified letter had been sent, the employee said he didn't receive it, nor was a receipt ever signed. And, anyone could have signed the receipt. This was a loop hole in the system. Domenick went to the Superintendent with this serious problem and asked permission to implement a solution to close this loop hole. He said that if he could send one of his Retention clerks to hand deliver the letter of a job offer, and get the employee's signature, this would validate the fact that the job offer had been received. Also, in the event the employee refused to sign for the letter, the department would have a signed statement from the Retention clerk that the letter was personally delivered. Domenick would use two of his most trusted and capable clerks for the job.

The Superintendent thought Domenick had a good solution to this problem. He said that he would have to bring the idea in front of the Admiral's Committee at the next meeting. By the end of the week Domenick had the decision he was waiting for. The decision had been made to go ahead with his plan as it was approved. There were many details to work out, but the two clerks Domenick selected were eager and willing to go. Within a month Domenick's plan showed positive results. The problem of employees eluding job offers, RIF, and grievances was ending. The Retention Department had developed a reputation of having a "Flying Squad." Some of the staff jokingly wore wings on their lapels. Domenick made other small changes which helped the Department run smoothly. These did not go unnoticed.

Frank Lisi, who was in charge of the Grievance Department, went to Superintendent Nat Doctors, and expressed that his department was experiencing a larger number of trivial grievances. The time consuming meetings with the union leaders of the various trades and fraternal organizations were burdensome. This problem had leaked out to Joe Bionjovani. Joe was a knowledgeable person, especially regarding field operations of the Navy Yard. He knew the various organizations in the Yard, and he knew that Domenick had been Secretary of the National Association of Government Employees of the AFL/CIO, treasurer of the Independent Welders of America, Vice President of the Columbia Association, and a member in other organizations. Bionjovani brought this fact to the attention of the Superintendent. The Superintendent asked Domenick if he would take some time in his busy day to help Frank Lisi, who was the nervous type, with any of Grievance Department meetings.

In effect Domenick would wear two hats. He would have two offices. One in the rear of the building, the Retention office, and another in front, which is the Grievance Department. He would in effect be Frank Lisi's assistant. As always, Domenick never said no. he said it would be a pleasure to work with Frank and deal with the various organizations. Domenick's intimate relationships with union leaders had developed when all of the organizations had worked together in a consortium. Domenick handled most of the meetings with organization leaders and resolved a great number of unwarranted grievances. This was a load off Lisi's mind and he was appreciative. He helped Frank with some of the Congressional inquiries. Frank also brought Domenick along whenever he had to attend administrative meetings. Meetings such as the Superintendent's Staff meetings or the Admiral's Committee meetings. Domenick witnessed many important decisions made regarding the base closure of the New Yok Naval Shipyard, commonly called the Brooklyn Navy Yard. Domenick's accomplishments were well known. His effective operation of the Retention department, the valuable assistance he gave to the Grievance Department, and his contributions at some meetings earned him a two-page "Superior Accomplishment Award" signed by the Superintendent, Nat Doctors, and Frank Lisi. This award was given to Domenick personally by Admiral Halzworth. The Admiral recognized Domenick immediately not only from some of his meetings with unions, but also for the "Admiral's Commendation Award" given to him after the heroics during the CVA-64 Constellation's horrendous fire. The Admiral not only shook his hand but even gave him a hug.

It is to be noted that during all this time the IRO personnel were working ten hours a day, six days a week. This was necessary to meet the one year deadline for the Navy Yard's closure. The work was hard and tedious but the money was good. To reflect back in time when Domenick was unemployed, he had applied with the City of New York for a Substitute Teacher's License. To obtain this license one had to go through the exact same testing and investigation as for a Regular Teacher's License. Domenick took the written test, subject performance test, oral interview, the demonstration of classroom technique by giving a short lesson to students, and finally, fingerprinted and photographed. After being investigated, Domenick passed all these rigorous tests and received his Substitute Teacher's License. This enabled him to substitute teach in any New York City school if and when called. The only difference between a Substitute Teacher and a Regular Teacher was that a regular teacher is appointed from a competitive list and is given a permanent assignment. A Substitute teaches only when on-call. If a Substitute happens to teach every day for a whole year, then they are called a Permanent Substitute Teacher.

It is always the hope that a Substitute will get on the competitive list. If this happens then the time spent substituting counts towards retirement and seniority.

Domenick did substitute at Eli Whitney High School in Brooklyn a few times. But when Nancy called him for the clerk's job in the Navy Yard, he put the idea of teaching aside. The Substitute teacher License did give Domenick an opportunity to register for evening tuition free classes at the New York Teachers Education School, which ironically was housed on East 9th Street in one of the New York University buildings. If one had a four year apprenticeship in a specific trade, plus five years working in that trade, they could attend these classes. It is also ironic that when Domenick was an Instructor of Apprentices in the Navy Yard he applied to this school a few times and each time was turned down. Now that he has his New York City Substitute Teacher's License he is accepted. This circumstance made it look like they were prejudiced against Federal employees.

Well, no matter, Domenick attended evenings at the Teachers Education School. If one completes the required evening course of 30-credits, which took about two years, the individual was certified by the New York Education Commission to teach his trade subject, in Domenick's case, Welding technology anywhere in New York State, except New York City. The City had their own requirements, as previously described for Domenick's Substitute Teacher License. The State Commission certifies teachers, whereas the City's Board of Education licenses teachers. There is a difference between Certification and Licensing.

Domenick welcomed attending the evening classes two nights a week. Although driving from Queens to Brooklyn in heavy traffic and working ten hours a day six days a week was exhausting, he never complained or missed a day from this tough routine. His social life was nil, as he buried himself in school assignments and studies. Even with this strenuous lifestyle, Domenick never neglected his family. Whenever a need arose for Vickie, his children, or close relatives, he somehow was always there. His motivation, determination and stamina made everything appear normal. Creating the illusion that abnormal appears normal was a trick Domenick tried to achieve. Did he succeed? Only his family and friends could answer that question.

Time rapidly passed and it was getting close to the Navy Yards closure date. Many of the IRO personnel started leaving, either for other jobs or to register with the Employment Office. There was one department which was to be saved for possibly another six months. This was the Safety Department, which was handling all compensation claims, and there were thousands of these claims. The department was to be moved over to the Naval Applied Science Laboratory. The Lab was a large complex next to the Navy Yard, and they gave an entire floor space in one of their buildings to house the Safety Department. A new name was given the Safety Department: Residual Compensation Claims Department. All of the career Safety officers were gone. The Compensation Claims Department now operated with a few career employees, but mostly with temporary employees. Mrs. Hennesy was a GS-9 Supervisor with career status. She could retire but was hanging on until the last minute. She was tough but fair.

She had approached Domenick and made him a job offer to come and work with the Claims Department. She knew his reputation as one who has the initiative and ability to get a job done. Domenick admitted he knew very little about the compensation process. She told him she knows he is a fast learner, and she knew he needed a job. Mrs. Hennesy mentioned that there were still career jobs outside the Defense Department freeze. These were posted at the "Lab," as it was called.

"You never know. You may still land a job back

with the Federal Government and restore your career status."

Domenick graciously thanked Mrs. Hennesy for her offer and accepted the position, which was still a GS-5. He asked for one favor, that he finish the job with Frank Lisi. She agreed that when the Navy Yard closed he could then report to the Claims Department at the Lab.

As the days were winding down the office equipment had to be labeled as to where it will be shipped. Frank and Domenick supervised this operation. When the movers came in and hauled everything out of IRO, the place looked big and barren. The last three men remaining in the vacant IRO building were Frank Lisi, Nat Doctors, and Domenick. It was eerie. Frank put a padlock on the main entrance door. Domenick kept a key as a memento. Superintendent Nat Doctors had tears in his eyes as he said goodbye to the two men and to the Navy Yard. A Navy Yard with 125 years of illustrious history, the second largest and most modern Navy Yard in the world, was now closed forever because of politics. It was a sad moment. It was strange that as Frank and Domenick went to their cars the sky darkened and it started to rain.

"This rain is for all the men who died working in this Navy Yard," Domenick said to Frank. It was a sad moment.

Domenick reported for work at the Naval Applied Science Laboratory at his appointed time. Mrs. Hennesy welcomed him and teamed him up with a knowledgeable person, who would show him the forms and procedures of the Claims Department. This knowledgeable person was a veteran of the Marine Corps. Her name was Sherry. She was very pretty, with red hair. She was scheduled to leave in two weeks for another position. Domenick had to learn her job in that two weeks and take over her duties. This was a typical situation as he was always put into tight spots. But he always prevailed.

Sherry was helpful but also very aggressive with her amorous gestures. She took a fancy to Domenick. He was flattered but her advances made him uncomfortable. He tried his best to be professional and ignore her advances, but there were many times she got angry at his "coldness." It was hard to be disinterested and keep a good working relationship with Sherry, yet he did succeed in developing a friendly relationship. He couldn't wait for the weeks to end and she would be gone. On the day she was leaving the job she put her telephone number and address in Domenick's jacket pocket. He naturally discarded it later.

The work schedule at "Claims" wasn't as hectic as was the Navy Yard. Personnel worked eight hours a day and only five days a week. Although Domenick could have used the overtime, he was happy for normal working hours. Decreased hours allowed Domenick to follow some of his neglected passions, working out at the YMCA, scuba diving, hunting, collecting military weapons, and gunsmithing. In between work and school he managed to go the YMCA and to, in a limited way, enjoy the other activities.

Domenick learned the workings of the Claims Department quickly. Being a quick learner he was able to work alone with no problem. In fact, Mrs. Hennesy gradually gave him more responsibility in adjudicating compensation claims. He began to communicate with the Regional Compensation Bureau concerning the more complicated cases. Dealing with this Regional office allowed him to talk with some important people, and those interactions developed into congenial working relationships. These relationships had benefits. Some people at the Bureau were made aware of Domenick's qualities and abilities. One day an adjudicating officer-in-charge said to him that there might be an opening for an Adjudicator GS-7, and if he was interested the officer would keep him in mind. This could be a good opportunity for Domenick to get back into Federal service and his career status. The only drawback was that the position is located in the Regional Office located at 48th Street in Manhattan. It would be a difficult trip to make from Bellrose. He couldn't use a car because of parking problems, so he would have to take a bus and then the subway. At the same time Domenick saw a position for Instructor of Vocational Subjects GS-7 posted on the bulletin board. It was with the National Park Service. Domenick filed for this position and was quickly notified to come in for an interview.

He went to the Regional Office in Manhattan and was interviewed by an Assistant Director. The interviewer was very impressed with Domenick's resume. He also said that Domenick made a favorable impression on him.

Domenick asked, "Who will I be teaching and where is the school located?"

With that the Director of the Regional Office joined in the interview. He took Domenick into a conference room and showed him a mock-up of a national park with various buildings and campsites. This park was located in New Jersey and had two connecting causeways, one to the Statue of Liberty and another to Ellis Island. The Director said when this park is completed it will be called Liberty national Park. He said that Domenick would be on the ground floor in its construction. Also, Domenick would be doing two important and altruistic things. One, helping teach 16 to 21 year old disadvantaged dropouts, and two, help build a national park on the waterfront in Jersey City. Domenick was very excited about this project and he accepted the position. The Assistant Director shook his hand and wished him luck.

Domenick couldn't wait to get home and tell Vickie and the children the good news. To travel to Jersey City didn't seem too bad. Domenick could use the car. He mapped out the route. From the Navy Yard it was a short distance over the Manhattan Bridge onto Canal Street and through the Holland Tunnel into Jersey City. The waterfront was just outside the Tunnel. Everything looked great on the surface. When Domenick went back to work at the Lab, he submitted his resignation. Everyone was happy for him. Mrs. Hennesy wished him the best of luck and said he would be sorely missed.

EIGHT
Job Corps

In 1966 Domenick received his letter of Appointment as an Instructor GS-7 with the Department of Interior's national Park Service. He was assigned to the Liberty Park Job Corps Center in Jersey City, New Jersey.

The Liberty Park Job Corps Center was one of many Centers established under President Johnson's "Great Society" program. The center had 24-hour accommodations for the 16-to-21y/o disadvantaged dropouts. They would be clothed in attractive work uniforms and fed the best nourishing food available. Their attendance would be strictly voluntary. The Center's mission was to educate these young people in the academic and vocational subjects necessary to complete a high school diploma. Also the young people will be taught good work ethics and work skills by working on various projects. As examples, at Yosemite National Park they worked on forest projects, and at Liberty Park they will help build the national Liberty Park connecting to the Statue of Liberty and Ellis Island. This program, if properly implemented, would be one of the best instruments to help young people create a good society and build a country all could be proud of. Domenick strongly believed in this philosophy to help young people. He was excited about this unique project.

Domenick reported to the Job Corps Center in a beautiful suit and ready to teach. To his surprise he found a long dirt road leading to the waterfront. At the end of the road were two pre-fabricated buildings. One large building was the administration building, and the smaller structure appeared to be a storage or work building. The surrounding terrain was barren except for overgrown weeds of the low lands. This land was to be reclaimed and have constructed on it an enormous national park. This appeared to be a formidable task, especially if the "Corpsmen," as the students were called, were the only ones doing the construction. This project looked like a job for real professionals, but time would tell. Domenick entered the administration building and observed that there were only five people in the large room. He saw the Director's office, the Assistant Director's office, and on the open floor three people worked at their desks. Domenick later learned the Assistant Director's name was John Ingram, a Black man. The Director's secretary was Black, and the two other workers, one male and one female, were White. The only people who were career employees were White, all others were political appointees.

Domenick walked up to the Black girl and said that he was the new Instructor reporting for duty. She took his appointment papers and told him to be seated. After a while she said the Director will see him shortly. While he sat patiently waiting to see the Director, a tall thin Black man came in and said, "Breakfast is ready." This fellow's name was Ben and he was one of the instructors, who was classified with a GS-9 rating. He was a political appointee. Ben's job every morning was to go into Jersey City for the mail and to buy donuts, cakes or bagels for the staff. Nice job. The Director finally came out to talk to Domenick. His first comment was, why are you all dressed up? Where are your work clothes? His tone was certainly not friendly but more condescending. Domenick was taken aback but politely came back with he was under the impression he was supposed to be teaching youngsters and not to be a laborer. With that the Assistant Director, John Ingram, came out of his office and said to the Director that there is some misunderstanding here and he will take care of this problem. The Director went back into his office and the Assistant Director apologized to Domenick for the Director's actions. John Ingram was more of a diplomat. His attitude was much better than the Director's. He was friendly toward Domenick and acted in a professional manner. He stated that the Director was under a lot of pressure and that there were no students here as yet. The students were scheduled to arrive when two Dormitory buildings and a Mess Hall were built. It should be soon as the private contractors could put up prefabricated buildings in no time. In the meantime if Domenick could lend his vocational expertise in helping the staff, who were working in the smaller building, it would be greatly appreciated. Domenick understood and being a flexible person cooperated. His old expression was you have to roll with the punches. He told the Assistant Director that he would gladly cooperate and pitch-in wherever necessary. While he remained in the main office the rest of the day, he found that the White girl handled personnel records among other things. Her name was Sherri McFadden. The White man handled, among other things, the payroll and the budget. His name was Joseph Shultz, Both of them were very friendly and tried to be helpful.

Domenick reported to the main office the next morning in his work clothes and then went directly to the small building to see what he could do. There was no supervisor anywhere. It appeared that everyone was doing their own thing. He saw a Black man cutting large bookcases in half with a power saw. In another room two Black fellows were sanding the finishes with power sanders. Domenick introduced himself and found the three men to be very friendly. They said they were salvaging the bookcases to be used later in the classrooms. They asked Domenick if he would help. He said yes and relieved the man who was doing the cutting. He suggested to the two men doing the sanding that they should wear masks or at least handkerchiefs over their mouths and noses, so as to protect them from the dust they were creating. They thanked him for thinking of them.

Slowly the buildings were being constructed, the Dormitories, the Mess, hall, an Academic Building, vocational building, and the storage building. More and more personnel were reporting to the Center. A great number were not qualified as they should have been, and many were political appointees. Domenick worked with many of these men redesigning floor plans, changing walls, doorways, putting up partitions, moldings and general repairs, and field projects. He became well respected by these men because of his knowledge and leadership qualities. The recently hired Superintendent of Maintenance approached Domenick and said that he could get him a Supervisor GS-9 position if he worked for him. Domenick respectfully declined saying he liked teaching and he was looking forward to the arrival of the young corpsmen, as the students will be called.

Finally the young students were arriving at the Center and things slowly began to get organized. The student population and their backgrounds were quite different than those found at any other Centers throughout the United States, They were mostly Black and from the inner city of New York. This also was true of most of the personnel at the Center. There were approximately 600 corpsmen at one time at the Center. More than 520 were Black, with the remainder Hispanic and White. Of 55 personnel, 43 were Black, 5 were Hispanic, and 7 White. Only 10 were career employees. The personnel consisted of the Director (Black), Assistant Director (Black), a secretary (Black), Personnel Clerk (White), a payroll and Budget Clerk (White), two Guidance Counselors (1 Black and one White), a principal (White), 4 Teachers (2 Black and 2 White), 2 Vocational Instructors (1 Black and 1 White), a Superintendent of Maintenance (Black), and 40 Work leaders (30 Black, 3 Hispanic, and 7 White). This recorded observation is not to project racism or discrimination, but to give a clear picture of the make-up at the Liberty Park Job Corps Center.

To give details of some of the functions of the Center are as follows. Domenick and Ben were supposed to work together and develop classes with vocational subjects designed to be coordinated with the Academic Department and Field Operations. Unfortunately, Ben still liked to be a deliveryman and bring mail and breakfast goodies to the Administration staff. He was rarely inside the Vocational building. It is to be noted that ben was GS-9, the Director's nephew, owned a Bar and Grill, and lived in a rent-controlled project with his mother, who was on welfare. The objective of the Vocational Department was to provide meaningful classes, but with Ben off somewhere, plus having limited equipment and supplies, it was a very difficult objective to accomplish. Domenick was frustrated. He was used to working in the Navy Yard, a Federal installation, where anything they needed to get a job done was provided. At the Job Corps Center, which was supposed to be a Federal installation, he was provided with limited resources. This was hard to understand. But as time went on he began to see the reasons why.

In the meantime he did the best he could. The Corpsmen who attended Domenick's basic mathematics and carpentry classes saw how he scrounged, manipulated, and pressured the administration and field work leaders to get what he needed. For example, in order to get equipment and supplies for the Metal and Welding Technology classes started, Domenick managed to convince the Maintenance Department to lend one of their portable gasoline power welding generators, which had to run outside and welding cables passed through a window, he also got from them a portable Flame Cutting rig. The proper way to conduct a Welding class is to have a welder for each student. But one machine was better than none. He pressured the Director, through the Principal, to requisition a couple of Welding Shields, spare glasses, safety glasses, welding jackets, welding gloves, and welding rods. For a supply of metal to be used by the students for practice and projects was out of the question.

When Domenick first came to the Center he spied an old abandoned ferry rusting on the beach nearby. Being an old sailor he boarded the vessel and checked her out. He remembered the ferry when he needed metal. He and a few of his Corpsmen wheeled and dragged the Flame Cutting rig through the dirt to the Ferry. Domenick proceeded to cut out large sections of metal. The Corpsmen carried the sections to the Vocational building. There Domenick cut the sections into long strips for the supply. Many Corpsmen witnessed this feat and word spread around about Domenick's dedication to have classes from which the students could benefit. Domenick built a welding bench and booth. He gave lessons in Welding, Cutting and Forming metal. He taught the theory associated with metal and metal forming. With these skills the Corpsmen love to make metal sculptures. The Superintendent was pleased to see his equipment being put to good use. He said to Domenick that the Field Department already benefited as welding jobs that were needed were performed by Corpsmen. If the Field Department had to contract out the jobs, it would cost a fortune. Domenick decorated the walls around the Welding section with the Corpsmen sculptures tagged with their names. He also decorated the rest of the building with appropriate pictures of projects. These impressed any visitors who came to the Vocational building.

The Field Department had the responsibility to put in sidewalks constructed of concrete, but it was decided to have temporary wooden walkways. The Regional Director of the National Park Service sent a memo saying that President Johnson and the Governor of New Jersey were coming to the Liberty Park Job Corps Center to christen its name. It was common practice for the President to visit each new Job Corps Center. Director Banks was in a tizzy. Straighten up, clean up, and hurry up was all everyone heard. He worried that the walk between buildings might be muddy. Why weren't the walkways completed? The reason was that the Work Leaders were working slow and constructing each 6-foot walkway on the ground. They would lay the 6-foot long 2'x4"s on each side of the walkway, lay a plank on top, and then nail the plank. They would have to square up the other end of the 6-foot walk before laying out all other planks to be nailed. This was slow and unproductive. These workers probably never saw a production line. Director Banks pressed the Superintendent to get the job done.

Domenick suggested to the Superintendent that if he would have the lumber and accessories sent over to the Vocational building, he would get the job done before the President's visit. The Superintendent believed in Domenick's ability and did what he said. Domenick designed a jig, as it is called, which could simulate a production line. He had the 6-foot 2"x4"s placed in the jig and the planks laid right on top of them. That way two Corpsmen, one on each side, could simply walk down and nail the planks in rapid succession. Domenick had three of these jigs operational with six Corpsmen eager to participate. This production line set-up could produce a quality 6-foot walkway every fifteen minutes. The entire job was completed in less than a week. Domenick and the Corpsmen were complimented by the Director and the Superintendent for a job well done.

Domenick always wanted to create a Drafting and Blueprint Reading class. The walkway feat enabled him to finally get approval by the Director to purchase six drafting tables with all its equipment and supplies. This seemed like a good reward for a job well done, but was this the way to get a class started for the benefit for the youngsters? The class should have been done automatically as part of the curriculum. Where was all this money going that is supposedly appropriated for the Job Corps Center? The Academic Department seemed to have no problems getting equipment or supplies, but then again it did not need much. Chalkboards, textbooks, workbooks, and visual aids were not too costly. Their priority is to get a Corpsman his G.E.D. diploma. The Vocational Department needed machinery, equipment, accessories, and supplies for the Corpsmen to acquire good work skills, and those were expensive. This was an area which should and possibly did have a great deal of money appropriated in the budget. Where is this money? Why did Domenick have to scrounge for everything Vocational needed? This caused Domenick to start to think, and many a night he spoke with his school friends at his evening classes. They too believed that something was definitely wrong. No one would say it was stealing, but...was it? It is to be remembered that Domenick was still attending evening classes at the New York Education School in Manhattan two nights a week.

President Johnson and the Governor were to arrive on Saturday at 10:00 A.M. Everyone was excited and thought that the entire staff from the Center would be invited. Domenick looked forward to attend this momentous occasion with his wife, Vickie. She was so excited she couldn't wait. The shock came when he found out that only certain employees were invited. This was an extremely depressing time for Domenick, especially seeing the Sunday newspaper with the Job Corps article showing the President, Governor, the Regional Director, Job Corps Director, the Superintendent, and Ben, in a group picture. This was so outrageous and upsetting that Domenick could not speak all day.

When he went back Domenick started to document and try to investigate the stories he heard about mismanagement, every rumor the Corpsmen were telling and the trucks that moved in and out of the supply building. In general he kept his eyes opened. It was getting cold and many of the Corpsmen had no field jackets. They wore sweaters or civilian jackets. Domenick inquired to the Supply Department about field jackets and the answer was they were coming. Domenick kept a watch. The jackets never came. He checked the dormitories and found old blankets that were not government issued. There were many improprieties in the Center's equipment. He saw field equipment that were second hand. A Broadhead and Garrett salesman named Frank Fasano had visited Domenick at the Vocational building hoping to sell some more equipment. Broadhead and Garrett was a company which sold a multitude of educational equipment to schools all over the country. Frank Fasano had a puzzled look on his face and he questioned Domenick when he saw the automotive stands.

"Where are the automobile engines?"

"Oh! That's what those stands are for?"

Frank also asked, where were the auto tools and accessories? Where was all the automotive equipment that was delivered to the Center last year? Domenick was dumbfounded. He didn't answer but he asked Frank a number of questions, which Domenick later recorded these answers in detail. He also recorded everything he heard, saw, or discovered.

Domenick made many friends at the Center, but there were two individuals with whom he had developed a close relationship. One fellow, whose name was Juan Citroen, had many conversations with Domenick and he revealed to him about numerous mistakes that were happening in the field. Another close friend was Steve Pulaski, a teacher in the Academic department. He was a very altruistic and dedicated individual who had served in the Peace Corps in the Dominican Republic. He was hoping to go into the Foreign Service Agency and go to Vietnam to help poor orphan children. Steve lived at the Center and spent almost 24 hours a day there. He saw many things that were wrong not only with the Academic Department but also in the operating of the after-hours activities for the Corpsmen at the Center. There were drugs and girls coming in after hours, and when reported, they were overlooked by the Administration. Domenick recorded all this information. If the incident with the President's visit plus the possibility of corruption at the Center wasn't bad enough, what really caused Domenick to go ahead and expose these activities was the racial groups that were coming to the Center to preach hate. One of these racial groups was called the Black Panthers, whose reputation for violence was well known. They were invited by Director Banks to speak to all of the Corpsmen at the sports building auditorium. This speech was made during the day, and all Corpsmen and employees were required to attend this presentation. The Black Panther speeches spread the most vicious lies about White people. They spoke for over an hour on a distorted history of the country, and said that Black people should riot and kill every White devil they can find. Domenick was fuming and he had to say something. He said to one of the White co-workers, how can we sit here and allow these inflammatory speeches to go on while we are on Federal land under the American flag? We are teaching our kids and students to be tolerant and get along, while these radical Blacks are teaching them to hate us.

His co-worker replied, "Do you want to keep your job, or worse do you want to die?"

Domenick reflected on all the boys, Black and White, he had straightened out. Some were hard core "gang bangers,' yet he influenced many of them to go straight. Besides teaching classes, he used to have long discussions about "life" with individuals and groups of Corpsmen. He never forgot one such Black Corpsman called John Benson. He was such a bad kid but he imprinted himself on Domenick and he was like his shadow. Wherever Domenick would go, he would be there. He was a rough kid who always smiled. One day he said to Domenick that his grandmother would like very much to meet him, and for him to have dinner with them. Domenick asked where he lived, and he said in lower Manhattan in the projects next to Chinatown. He really liked this boy and so he said all right. When he went home he told Vickie that some night he will go to this boy's apartment and have dinner with his grandmother. The boy had no mother or father and was raised by his grandmother. Vickie said it was fine with her. Benson told Domenick the time and place and his address.

That night Domenick went to Benson's home and rang the bell to his apartment. Benson came down from the 8th Floor in an elevator and met Domenick. Domenick said to Benson that he was worried about something happening to his 1967 red Mustang. Benson said, don't worry, I got you covered. He walked over to a group of young boys and told them to keep an eye on the car. It comforted Domenick to know his car was protected. He followed Benson into the elevator and they went up to the apartment. Benson's grandmother gave a long look at Domenick and then she hugged him. She said she was so grateful for him saving her grandson. She also said that all her grandson talks about is Mr. Scarlato this and Mr. Scarlato that. They sat down and ate a delicious dinner that surprised Domenick. She had cooked lasagna and meatballs with a healthy antipasto salad. He asked her where she learned how to cook Italian food so good. She said she was raised in Georgia and when she came to New York she had gotten a job with a Catholic parish in Little Italy. She had worked for this parish for more than twenty-five years. The parish was in walking distance of her home. She said she cooked this meal especially for him. When Domenick left, his car was right where he had left it and it was untouched. As he drove away he saluted the group of boys and they saluted back. It was a most memorable evening which Domenick never forgot.

He also never forgot when Benson came home from Marine Corps Boot Camp and especially came to the Job Corps Center to see him. Domenick was so thrilled to see Benson that he invited him to his home in Bellrose for a Sunday dinner. He wanted to see him once more before he reported back to his unit. He had the strange feeling that Benson would be going to Vietnam. Domenick explained this to Vickie and his daughters. Benson arrived at the Scarlato home on time. He looked so sharp in his Marine Corps green uniform. In one hand he had a large box of candy for Vickie and the girls, and in his other hand he had an L.P. record of Frank Sinatra. He knew Domenick liked Sinatra. Domenick until this day has this record. They had a wonderful dinner and everyone enjoyed Benson's company. When it was time for him to leave, Domenick shook Benson's hand and said, you can call me Domenick. Benson emphatically said, no, you are Mr. Scarlato.

Domenick came back to reality and tried to work with enthusiasm, but it seemed as though his heart was being torn out. There was much tension in the news about unrest among Blacks according to their leaders. Having experienced the Watts Riot, Domenick felt that he should keep his M-1 Carbine with its 30-round banana clip in the trunk of the Mustang until this supposed tension subsided. One afternoon there came an announcement over the loud speaker that there was rioting in Newark and Jersey City. The cities were being looted, cars overturned, and buildings burning. Domenick said this is Watts all over again. He knew that if he stayed at the Center, especially after the session of the Black Panthers trying to stir up the young Black students, there was no telling what might happen. There was only one dirt road in and out of the Job Corps Center. Domenick opened the Mustang's trunk and took out his M-1 Carbine and loaded the weapon. He said, one way or another I'm getting home. There were four White Corpsmen who were scared out of their wits. They said to Domenick that the past few days some of the Black kids were beating up on the White kids. They asked Domenick to please take them home. Three lived in Manhattan and one lived in Brooklyn. Domenick said all right and they piled into the car. When Domenick had to go down one of the devastated streets to get to the Holland Tunnel, a group of thugs were obstructing their passage. Domenick drove slowly and made sure they could see the M-1 with its banana clip. They moved aside and allowed the Mustang to go through untouched. It was like Moses parting the Red Sea. After he safely drove each kid home, he headed quickly for Bellrose. Vickie and the children were so relieved when he made it home safely. They all hugged and kissed. The next day Domenick called in to the Job Corps Center and asked for the rest of the week off. It was granted. When he returned to work he was shocked to find one of the dormitories completely burned down. Thank God no one had been hurt.

All these events were too much for Domenick to bear. He said right then and there that the Job Corps Center had to go. Maybe other Job Corps were good, but this one was contaminated with Black racism and corruption by its leaders. This was proven by the Black panthers and other radical groups who were invited to brainwash and inflame the young Black students. And, the underhanded corruption had been observed and recorded. Also another fact not mentioned was the nepotism practiced at the Center. There were a number of employees who were related, a prime example being Ben, the Director's nephew. All of this completely violates federal law. Domenick went home and drafted a twelve page report detailing every illicit aspect that was occurring at the Center. After typing this report, Vickie said, you are working yourself out of a job, or worse, you may get killed. Domenick said that in good conscience he could not let this go on. He didn't sign the Report with his name. He signed it, "A very concerned career employee." He wiped each page clean of fingerprints. He then mailed it from a New Jersey post office. He sent copies to the regional Director of the National Parks Service, the Secretary of the Department of Interior, to the Senate Investigating Committee, and to the President of the United States.

Within a month the Center was visited by two regional Evaluators, supposedly to evaluate the progress of the Job Corps Center. They went around the Center making various inquiries. They asked employees questions about their activities, and also asked Corpsmen questions. When they came to Domenick, they asked general questions about the Vocational Department's activities and his role as an Instructor. He answered them in educational terms and listed the benefits the Corpsmen derived out of attending classes. Domenick knew by the tone and wording of some questions they were not to evaluate but investigate facts that his "Report" alluded to—and who may have mailed the Report. These men were not Regional Evaluators but Agents from some investigations Department. Within a short time a team of Investigators were going through the Administration Building and the Supply Building. It did not take long before the Director Al Banks and six other men were indicted for fraud, corruption, and a host of other charges. The Liberty Park Job Corps Center was to be closed in sixty days. Employees who were appointees were given thirty-day Notice of Termination, and career employees were given a sixty-day notice. All employees were responsible to help make the departure of the Student/Corpsmen as smooth as possible. They were also ordered to secure and label all equipment, and in general work towards the Center's closing.

It is unfortunate that a beautiful concept of creating a National Park where people could picnic, camp, and walk to the Statue of Liberty or Ellis Island, was shattered. If this Park had been administered by professional career employees it would have been completed and it would have flourished. Because of politics and corrupt men that dream was forever forgotten. A year later, after attending one of his evening classes, Domenick took a drive to see what had happened to the Liberty Park Job Corps Center. Upon arriving he saw a tall chain-link fence surrounding the entire property. At the entrance was a large sign which read, "The New Jersey State Drug Rehabilitation Center." Domenick wiped tears from his eyes and went home.

Domenick sacrificed fifteen years of federal service by uncovering a den of thieves. Now he is faced with choosing one of two roads to follow.

Should he try to follow his fifteen year career with the federal government? Or, does he try to pursue a long road for a career in education? Which one of the two roads will he follow? Only time will tell.

Made in the USA
Middletown, DE
14 October 2020